The architecture of

skyscrapers

Skyscrapers

AUTHOR
Francisco Asensio Cerver

EDITORIAL MANAGER
Paco Asensio

PROJECT COORDINATOR
Anna Puyuelo Abad (Architect)

TEXT
Michael Webb

DESIGN AND LAYOUT
Mireia Casanovas Soley

PHOTOGRAPHERS

Richard Davies, Ian Lambot (Commerzbank); Taizo Furukawa, Osamu Murai, C. Pelli, Yukio Yoshimura (Sea Hawk Hoteland Resort); Kouji Okamoto (Osaka World Trade Center); T.R. Hamzah & Yeang Sdn. Bhd. (Menara Budaya); T.R. Hamzah & Yeang Sdn. Bhd. (Central Plaza); José Moscardi Júnior (Plaza Centenario); Tomio Ohashi (Melbourne Central); Steinkamp/Ballogg Chicago (Jin Mao Building); Edge Media NYC (Shanghai World Financial Center); Murphy/Jahn (21st Century Tower); Murphy/Jahn (The Endless Towers and Brancusi Tower); Murphy/Jahn (Generale Bank Tower); Dennis Gilbert (DG Bank Frankfurt); Mitsuo Matsuoka, Kaneaki Monma, C. Pelli (NTT Headquarters); Osamu Murai (OUB Center); Roco Design Limited (Citybank Plaza); Richard Bryant/Arcaid, Jen Fong, Neil Troiano (Suntec City); Robert Royal (Torres Puerta de Europa); David Cardelús, David Manchón, James H. Morris, Anna Puyuelo (Hotel de les Arts); Osamu Murai, Shinkenchiku Shashinbu (The New Tokyo City Hall Complex); Tomio Ohashi, Anna Puyuelo (Umeda Sky Building); J. Apicella/CP&A, P. Follett/CP&A (Petronas Towers).

First published in 1997 by Arco for
Hearst Books International
1350 Avenue of the Americas
New York, NY 10019

Distributed in the U.S. and Canada by
Watson-Guptill Publications
1515 Broadway
New York, NY 10036

Distributed throughout the rest of the world by
Hearst Books International
1350 Avenue of the Americas
New York, NY 10019

1997 © FRANCISCO ASENSIO CERVER

ISBN: 0-8230-0255-

PRINTED IN SPAIN

Skyscrapers

Skyscrapers are a celebration of technological advances and a proud reflection of the human ability to create ever higher constructions. However, they are also a product of planning regulations, of the property market, and of speculation. Due to the astronomical price that land fetches in the center of cities, skyscrapers represent the ultimate form of urban investment.

Expertise in building skyscrapers has accumulated over time, but the basic questions confronting architects today are the same as those encountered by the designers of the first skyscrapers in Chicago at the end of the 19th century. What should be the relationship of the skyscraper with an urban context that is of a different scale? How should the building meet the ground? What is the most suitable structure and how should it be fortified against the elements?

Today's architects are at least conscious of urban problems as they design skyscrapers, and try, with greater or lesser success, to provide solutions to some of the problems that skyscrapers cause. The image of the skyscraper has undergone many changes over the passage of time, influenced of course by changes of taste and style and above all by the constant development of building techniques, making possible the construction of projects unimaginable until now.

As the designs presented in this book demonstrate, the morphology of this architectural typology has become ever more variable—monolithic towers, the articulation of the prism in sections of varying heights as a response to concrete requirements, and finally, double towers which, connected or not, form pairs representing a singular and unique image in the urban landscape.

The image presented by these buildings continues to set standards for an architectural type that from its beginning has been indissolubly linked to economic market forces and the symbolic representation that such forces demand.

Commerzbank

FRANKFURT, 1997

The new Commerzbank headquarters building is the most important development undertaken in Frankfurt in the last few decades. Foster & Partners have worked in close collaboration not only with the client, but also with the city planning authorities, to harmonize the development of this complex project with the community. This is one of the first examples of a skyscraper designed according to ecological criteria. Each individual office is designed so as to have natural ventilation. The building features spacious garden patios adorning the entire height of the building.

The relationship with surrounding buildings has been of prime importance in the project. The office tower has become an unavoidable reference point of the Frankfurt skyline. Situated in the center of Frankfurt, near the River Main, the site occupies a city block that includes housing on the southwest side and also the former Commerzbank headquarters tower. A sense of scale has been restored to the neighborhood by means of a low building that houses parking places and apartments on the Kirchnerstrasse side of the site.

To cushion its impact on the urban context, the tower hides behind existing buildings and the new apartment block. Only on the north side, where the main entrance is located, does the tower stand fully exposed. The site includes a new glass-enclosed public space that houses restaurants, cafés, and art galleries. In contrast to the tower that formerly served as the bank's headquarters, the new building responds to its urban surroundings, both in the decomposition of masses in the lower part of the complex and in providing public services. This rich and varied mixture of uses reflects the complexity of Frankfurt itself.

Detail of the façade of the final model.

Models used for preliminary studies of the tower's mass, with variations.

The 60-story tower reaches almost 300 meters, and is crowned by a telecommunications aerial. The triangular floor plan has gently curving sides so as to maximize the efficiency of the space. The organization of the structural part of the building is of vital importance to its success. Designed by the London engineering studio of Ove Arup, it is based on pillars that enclose the vertical communications and service nuclei at the corners of the tower. The pillars support Vierendel beams that cover the office space, making intermediate supporting pillars unnecessary. The exterior of the tower leaves the structural parts of the building exposed. The façade is self-supporting, and is composed of curtain walls of gray aluminum with windows that open. The pillars, covered in white aluminum sheets, frame the façade and define the overall mass of the building.

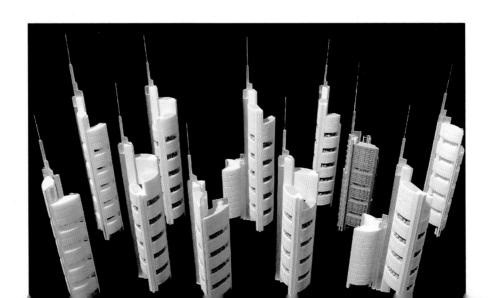

View of the roof of the final model. The immense pillars in the corners of the triangle support the Vierendel beams.

Floor plan of the fifth story. The lower floors of the building respond to the city environment around them, completing the perimeter of the block where it faces Kirchnerstrasse.

A diagonal pathway links Kaiserplatz with the busy Grosse Gallusstrasse to the north, creating a space that is open to the city.

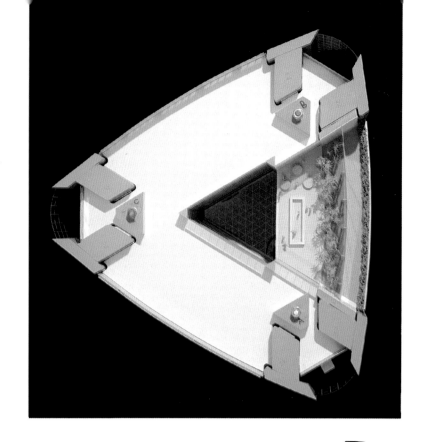

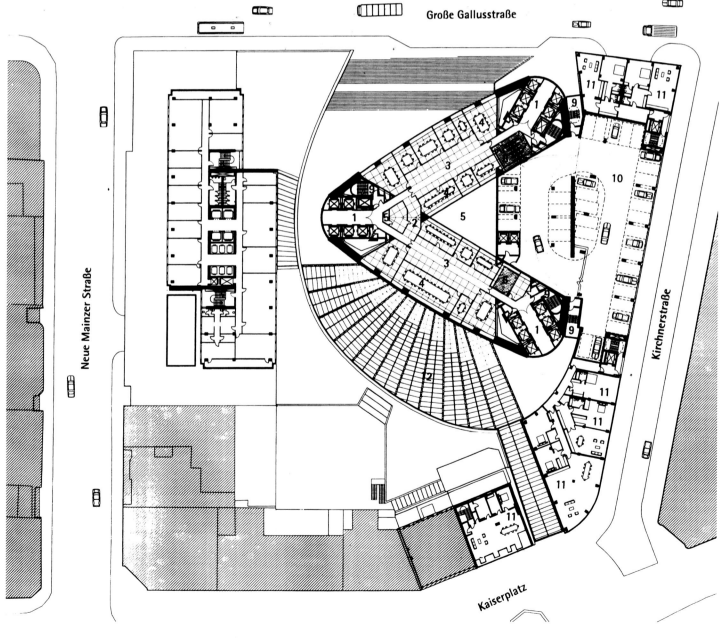

Typical office floor. The offices whose façade looks over the central atrium have a view of the city through the conservatories.

Floor forty-eight. The placing of the vertical communications and service nuclei in the corners facilitates communication between the offices and the patios.

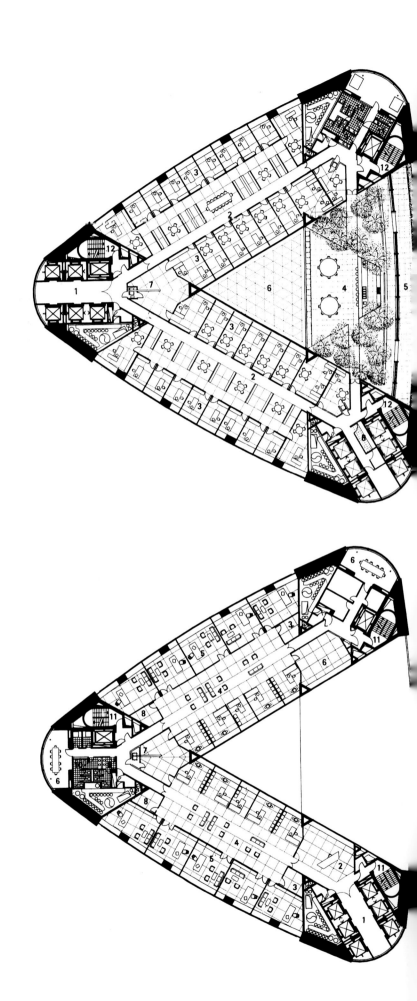

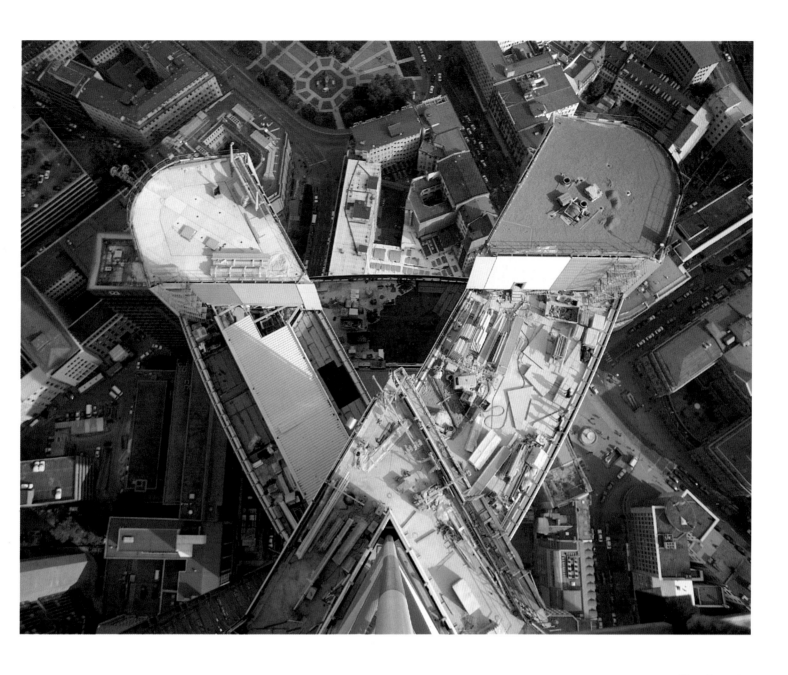

View from the
telecommunications aerial, still
under construction.

At night, the artificial lighting of the offices allows the interiors of the conservatories to be clearly seen.

Plan of the layout of the atrium which functions as a funnel. The conservatories help ventilate the offices in the interior of the building.

Detail of the façade. A curtain wall combines aluminum and windows that open to allow natural ventilation of the offices.

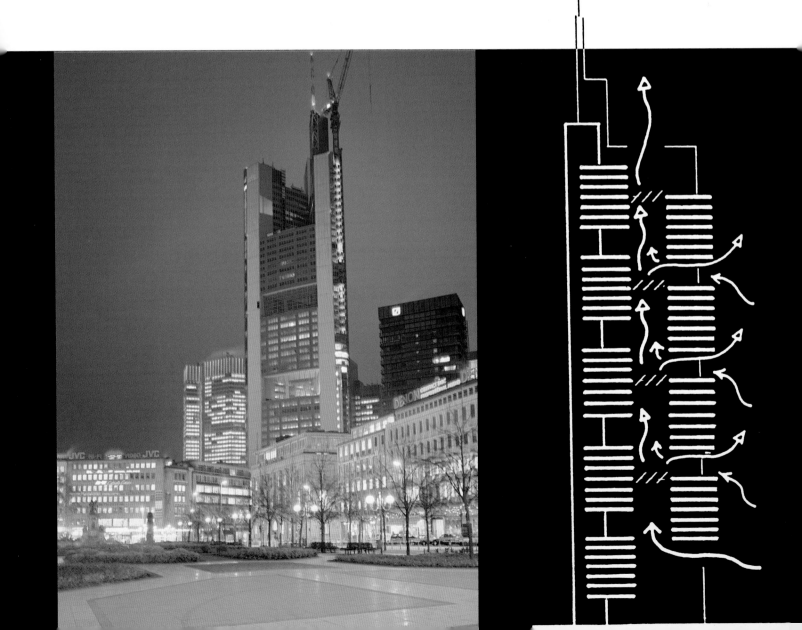

The self-supporting glass façade
of the conservatories, seen
while under construction.

The large atrium, reaching up through the whole building, allows natural ventilation of the interior façades, which receive light from two sides through the conservatories.

The glassed-in gardens improve the visual quality of the workspace and give perspective to the silhouette of the city seen beyond.

Sea Hawk Hotel and Resort

FUKUOKA, 1995

Cesar Pelli's designs share a common feature, which is an absence of preconceived ideas. Each project is designed according to place, climate, and culture; in other words, respecting the local environment. Using a wide range of strategies and materials, Pelli identifies and enhances the social value of the buildings he designs in an attempt to link esthetic value with social aspects. The volumes of his architectural designs always have a strong, defined shape. Materials are exploited to the limit of their color and expressiveness, erupting into the urban space with special character and personality. Built on the seashore, the Sea Hawk Hotel, which is visible from Fukuoka, soars up like a lighthouse, creating a composition of sculptural forms in Hakata Bay. The curves of the roof and the walls form a relationship with the elemental forces of wind and water. The complex is formed of three distinct volumes. Unlike occidental hotels, major hotels in Japan host activities such as wedding banquets, and include luxury restaurants, bars, clubs, shops, and conference facilities. These functions are as essential as that of providing accommodations to overnight guests.

The Sea Hawk Hotel and Resort was conceived primarily as a hotel for tourists. Its design responds to the special conditions of the area, the existing structures, and above all to the nature of Japanese hotel building. The modern city of Fukuoka includes the historic center of the city of Hakata, which has great historical value in Japan. The modern port, with its important tradition of fishing and sea-borne commerce, reinforces the symbolic links the city has with the sea.

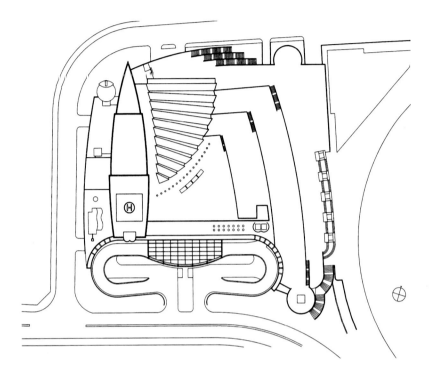

The 34 floors of the tower, whose floor plan is boat-shaped, house the 1,052 rooms, and enjoy impressive views of the sea. The new hotel is sited next to a baseball stadium with a capacity of 40,000. The walls are finished with ceramic tiles which form a rich texture of varying colors and designs. The motifs and curves soften the weight of the structure and reinforce the sensation of movement, in consonance with the wind and water.

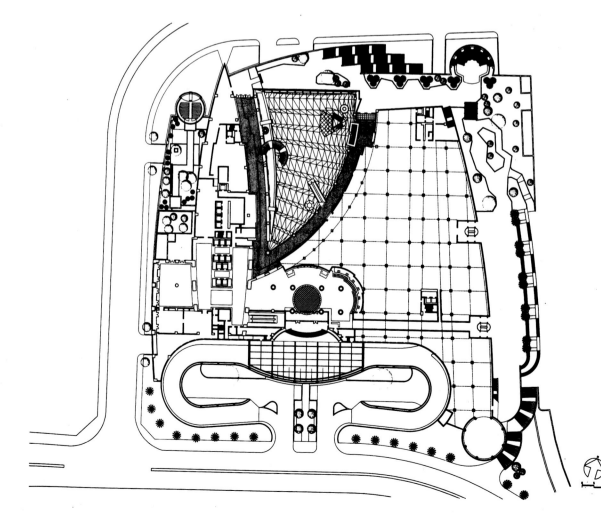

The spectacular volume of the atrium, in the shape of a horn, houses trees and fountains, and forms an urban plaza.

In addition to the trees and fountains, other elements in the atrium also receive a sculptural treatment, which culminates in an elevated platform known as the Treehouse from which visitors can enjoy views both of the sea and of the atrium.

View of the tower, which with
its "prow" open to the sea,
houses the rooms of the hotel.

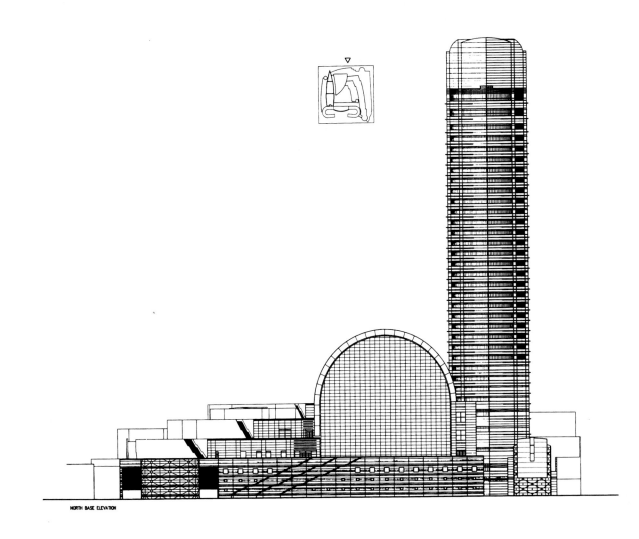

NORTH BASE ELEVATION

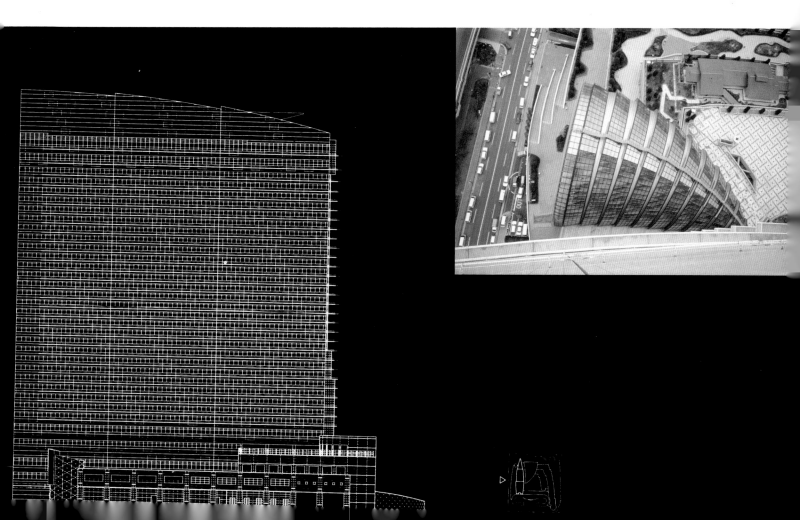

The walls are finished with ceramic tiles, forming a rich texture of different colors and designs.

Access stairs to the garden terraces.

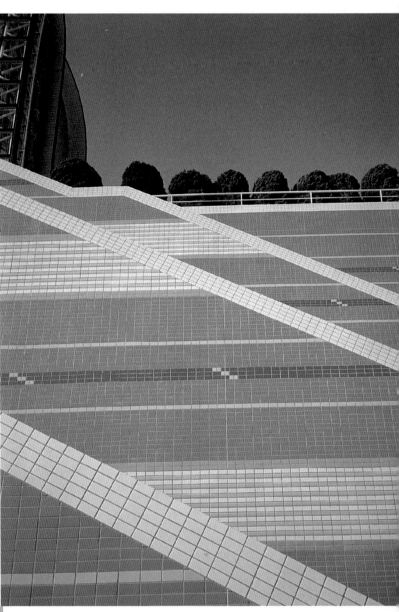

The volumes of Pelli's designs always have a strong and well-defined shape; the materials are used to the limit of their color and expressiveness, erupting into the urban space with a special character and personality.

Osaka World Trade Center

OSAKA, 1995

Technoport Osaka, where the Osaka World Trade Center is located, is a new urban center currently under construction in the Bay of Osaka. When finished, it will cover 775 hectares of land, divided into three artificial islands. Rising 256 meters high and with a surface area of more than 150,000 square meters distributed among its 55 floors, the Osaka World Trade Center—the highest building in the west of Japan—has in a short time become not only a symbol of the coastline where it is located, but also a visual landmark for the Bay, and the entire Kansai region.

The project incorporates various public spaces in its interior, opening it up to the general public and not just to those associated with the office portion of the project. An immense 3,000-square-meter atrium known as Fespa serves as the access point both to the principal vertical communications point of the tower and to the various public service areas, such as shops, restaurants, cafés, and an auditorium with a capacity of 380. All is contained within a global design that envisages the area as a major park. The atrium not only serves the building itself, but also integrates the complex with its urban surroundings, both in function and in scale.

The atrium, as well as serving as the access to the tower, captures the scale of Cosmo Square.

Floor plan of office floors 6-38.

Floor plan of office floors 39-49.

Floor plan of the panoramic gallery. Oriented according to the four cardinal points, it is rotated 45 degrees with respect to the tower.

Transversal section of the building.

At night, the WTCO appears as a great tower of light, with the observation deck in the crown.

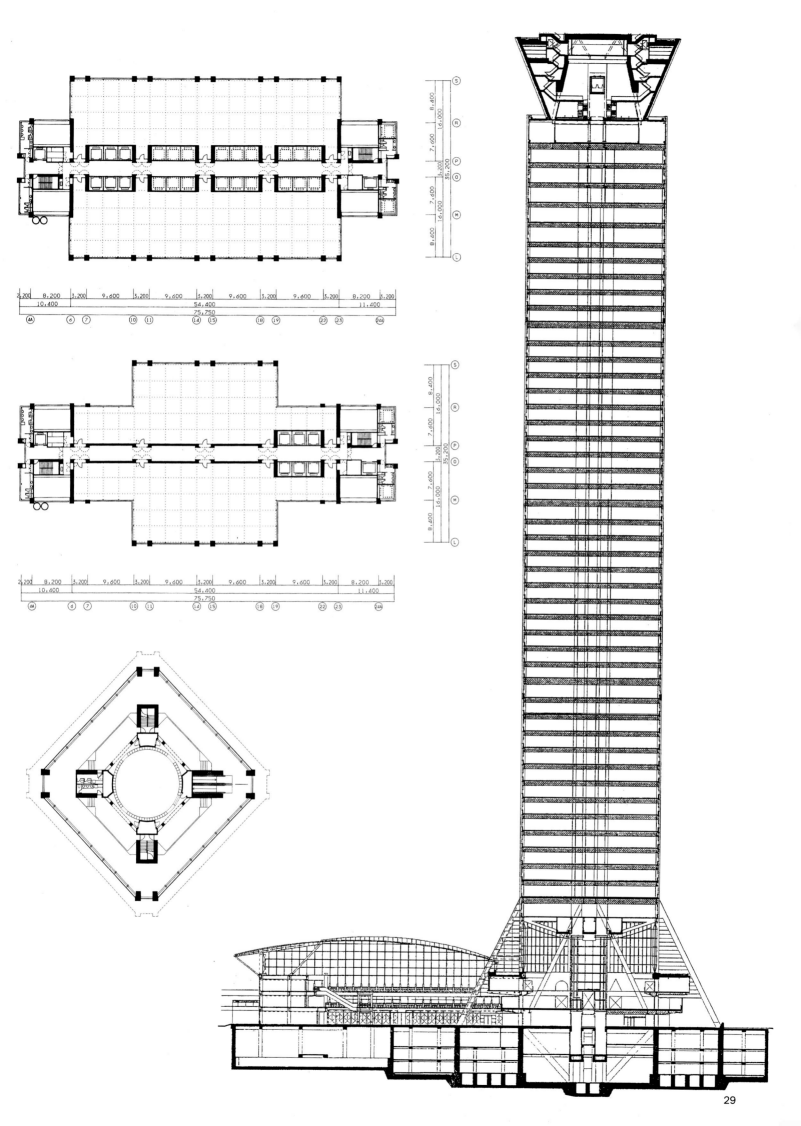

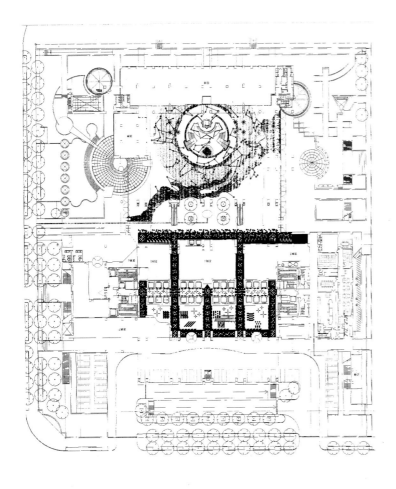

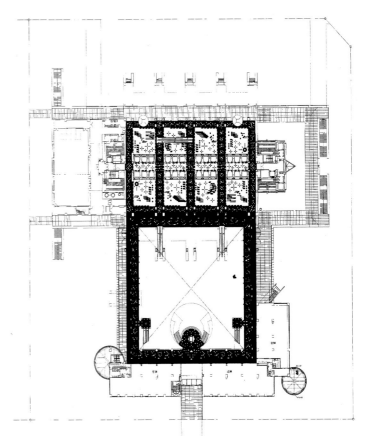

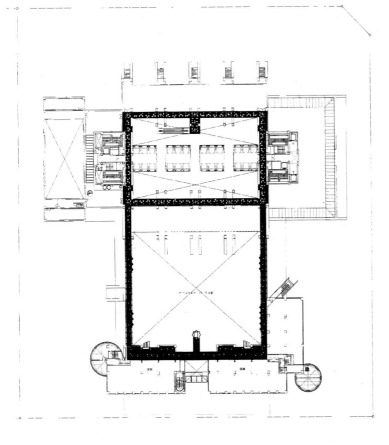

Ground floor, ground level.
Great entrance atrium.

First floor. Main access to the
elevator node.

Second floor.

Fespa, the huge central space. Because of its size, it is able to host large events.

The feet which support the tower shelter a lobby for the elevators.

Other public areas are located at the top of the building, from the forty-fifth floor upwards, leaving floors 1 to 44 occupied by offices. These are equipped with highly sophisticated computerized systems, including independent air-conditioning on each level and floors built to withstand the weight of mainframe computers. The floors beneath the crown of the tower incorporate a facility for wedding banquets, various restaurants, and the WTCO Museum. However, what undoubtedly draws the most attention is the pyramidal shape of the crown of the tower, which houses an observation post at the highest point of the bay.

The nucleus of elevators,
whose transparency permits a
complete view of the interior.

The structure of the underground part of the building is of reinforced concrete resting on a pile foundation that reaches down more than 60 meters. Above ground, a steel structure is used, among other reasons for its lightness and slenderness. The building incorporates the most modern technology available at the moment of construction, especially with regard to air-conditioning systems, and state-of-the-art computerized support systems. The visual comfort of the work area has also been taken into account, with large windows occupying the entire floor space, thus guaranteeing panoramic views of the bay for the workers.

Access corridor to the elevators.

The WTCO Club.

The large observation point on
the top floor allows the whole
Bay of Osaka to be seen.

Office working area, with views
over the bay.

Menara Budaya

Kuala Lumpur, 1992–1996

The Malaysian capital of Kuala Lumpur, where the Menara Budaya is located, lies just 3.7 degrees north of the Equator. The design of the building was constrained by the fact that the site is a rectangular parcel with its longest diagonal oriented north-south and that the design has to align itself with the neighboring buildings. The main axis deviates by 36 degrees from the north-south. As a result, the orientation of the façades is not ideal with respect to climatic conditions for a building situated so near the Equator.

Ken Yeang and Tengku R. Hamzad, two Malaysian architects specializing in the design of tall buildings, have written and lectured around the world on how to be sensitive to the environment and to energy consumption in tropical zones.

Given the building's unfortunate northeast-southeast alignment, the architects decided to round its corners. This resulted in a decrease in the surface area of the exterior façade and an increase in the wall area oriented north and south, which needs no protection from the sun. This decision meant that it was also possible to avoid the brutal contrast in temperatures that occurs between two façades at right angles, one in shadow and the other exposed to the tropical sun.

The system for ventilating the car-parking area is ingenious and efficient. The white strips of the lower building reflect the sun's rays, warming the air, which then ascends the façade, creating a convection current that is captured by the horizontal openings of the parking structure and serves to freshen the air inside the building.

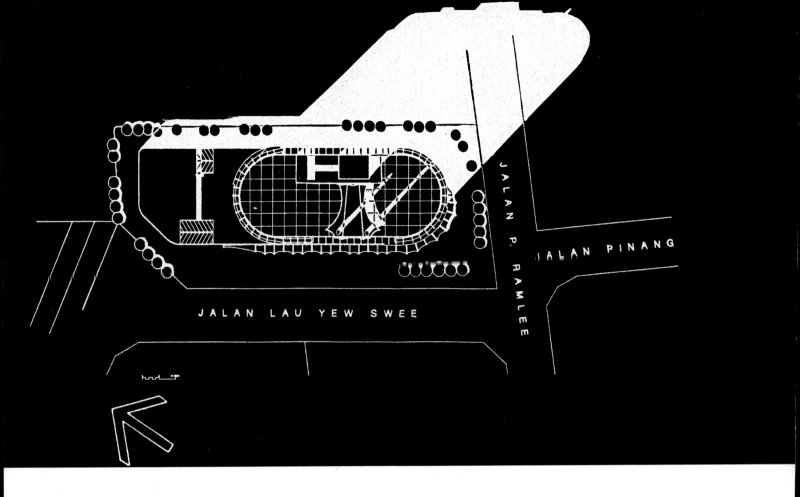

JALAN PINANG

JALAN P. RAMLEE

JALAN LAU YEW SWEE

This same technique is repeated within the tower itself, using the contrast between the dark glass skin of the exterior of the offices and the white finish of the lower building to create a current. The tension between the stereotype of an office block and the mechanisms by which that stereotype is distorted in the interest of efficient energy use is one of the most surprising aspects of the Menara Budaya, setting it apart from the buildings surrounding it.

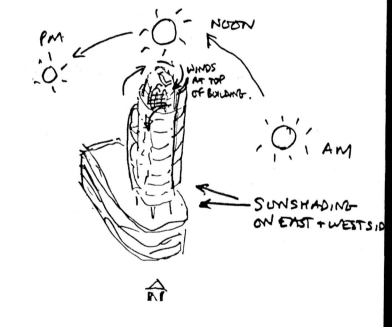

Plan of the siting of the building with a study of the projection of maximum shadow in the late evening.

Drawings and plans showing how the sun's trajectory affects the formal definition of the building.

Ground floor of the Menara Budaya showing the entrance lobby, the parking ramp, and the service areas.

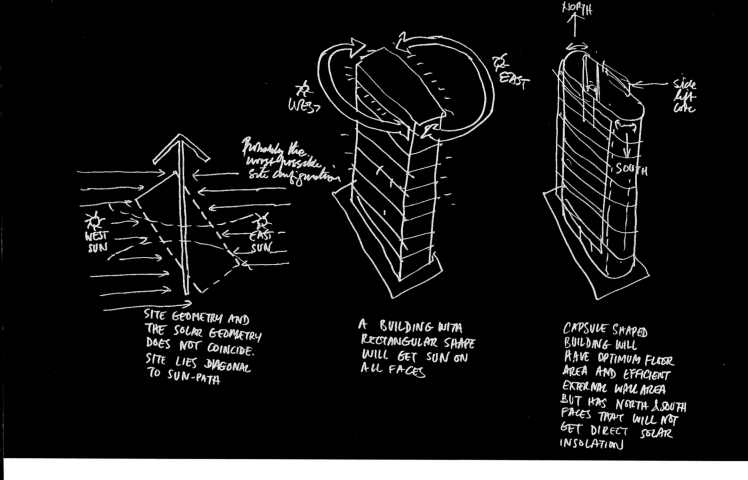

SITE GEOMETRY AND THE SOLAR GEOMETRY DOES NOT COINCIDE. SITE LIES DIAGONAL TO SUN-PATH

Probably the worst possible site configuration

WEST SUN

EAST SUN

to WEST

to EAST

A BUILDING WITH RECTANGULAR SHAPE WILL GET SUN ON ALL FACES

NORTH

side lift core

SOUTH

CAPSULE SHAPED BUILDING WILL HAVE OPTIMUM FLOOR AREA AND EFFICIENT EXTERNAL WALL AREA BUT HAS NORTH & SOUTH FACES THAT WILL NOT GET DIRECT SOLAR INSOLATION

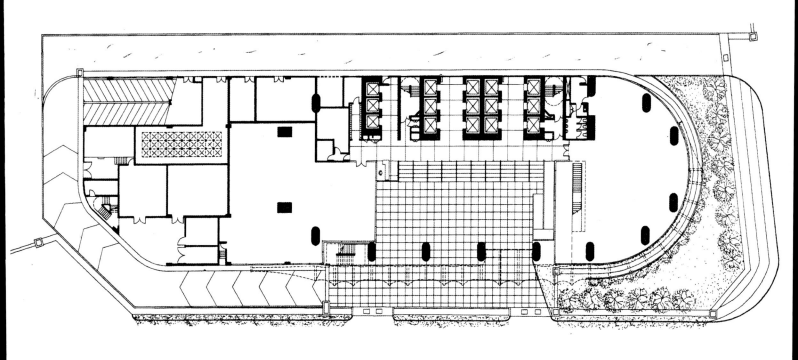

A 37-story office block, with a surface area of 66,442 square meters, the Menara Budaya is divided into two parts: a slender tower of dark glass designed to serve as office space, and a lower 7-story building serving as support for the tower and used as parking space for the office workers. The nucleus of the building (containing a small lobby, restrooms, elevators, emergency stairs, and other service areas) has been placed in the northeast façade, so that the horizontal rays of early morning sun do not disturb the office space, and so that the working space remains free of obstacles.

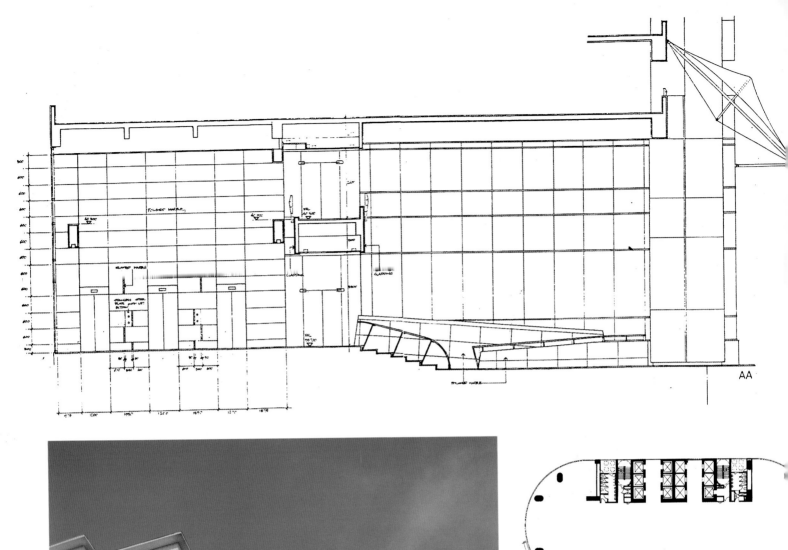

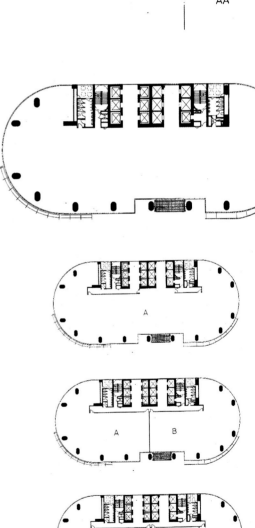

Front and side faces of the
entrance lobby showing the
quartering of the dressing
of fiery marble and
aluminum.

Perspective of the building
from the avenue showing
how the exterior shape of
the building contrasts with
its neighbors.

Floor plan of the office
block showing the different
possibilities for
compartmentalizing

Lateral view of the main
entrance with the awnings
that protect it and the
emergency stairs of the
parking structure.

View of the main façade
showing the recess that
runs right up it and the
crowning marquee.

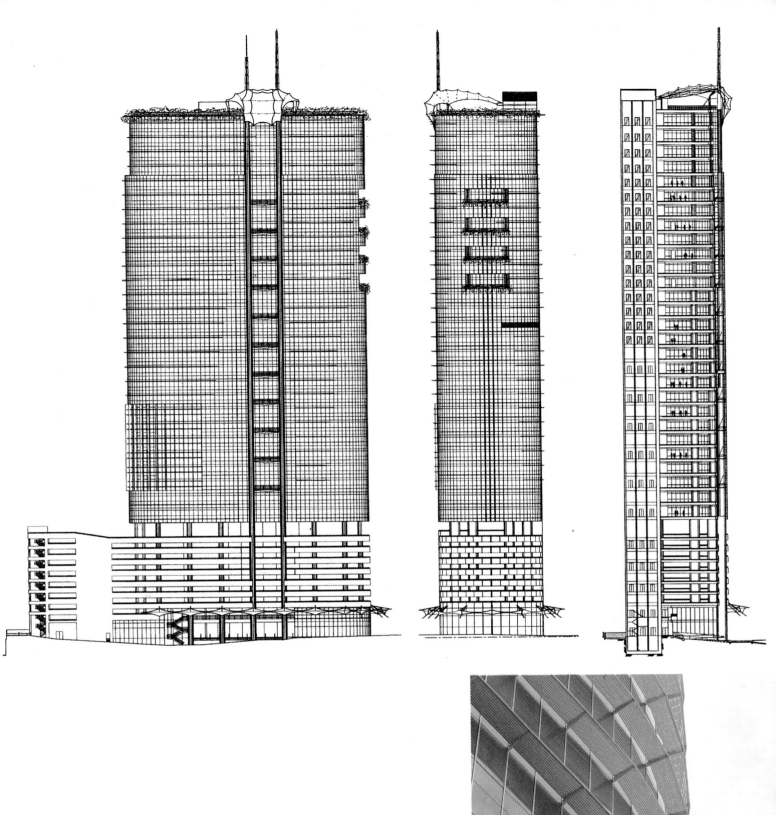

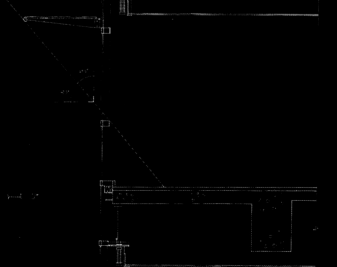

Face of the main façade: the continuity of the two pillars of the recess attempts to unify the different parts of the building.

Southeast face showing the interruption of the façade on the upper floors to allow for the small plant-filled terraces.

Transveral section through the atrium, showing how the service nucleus oriented toward the northeast is clearly differentiated from the office space.

Where necessary the façade is protected from the fierce sun by parasols.

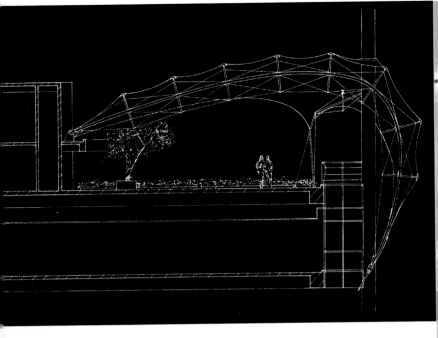

The profile of the marquee, constructed with stressed membranes of textile, provides an airy, shady space on the roof.

The unusual shape of the stressed membrane has vague echoes of ancient Malay temples.

The terrace has been designed to offer the office workers a spectacular view of the city.

Central Plaza

Kuala Lumpur, 1996

The great care taken in resolving the problems posed by the tropical climate of Kuala Lumpur has meant that what in principle was a monolithic prism has been softened and offers different faces giving a richer vision of the building's place in the urban context. This concept not only affects the building's external image but also leads to a more efficient use of energy. This bioclimatic approach tries to improve the comfort of the user in all senses. The requirements of the design were simple—space for offices and sufficient parking space for the office users.

The greatest architectural interest of the design lies in the various manipulations performed on the basic, narrow prism. The initial volume, heavily constrained by the shape of the site and also by structural limitations with respect to the horizontal force of typhoon-strength winds, necessitated sway-bracing of the block. This was achieved by concentrating all the necessary braces on the exterior of the walls, thus guaranteeing the stability of the structure and contributing to the appearance of the exterior.

To avoid an excess of tropical sunlight, the working space in the offices is oriented toward the north, with the façade being stepped back progressively until reaching the terrace. On each floor, potted plants climb the façade until they meet the vegetation surrounding the swimming pool, thereby forming a green fringe breaking the monotony of the smooth face of the façade.

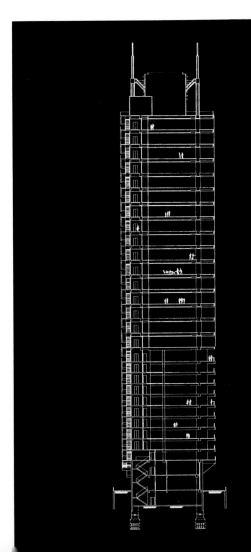

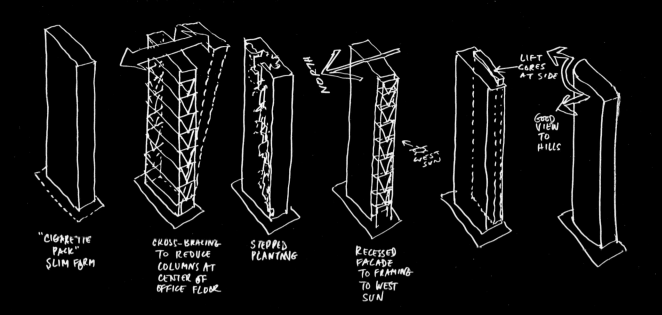

"CIGARETTE PACK" SLIM FORM

CROSS-BRACING TO REDUCE COLUMNS AT CENTER OF OFFICE FLOOR

STEPPED PLANTING

RECESSED FACADE TO FRAMING TO WEST SUN

LIFT CORES AT SIDE

GOOD VIEW TO HILLS

NORTH

WEST SUN

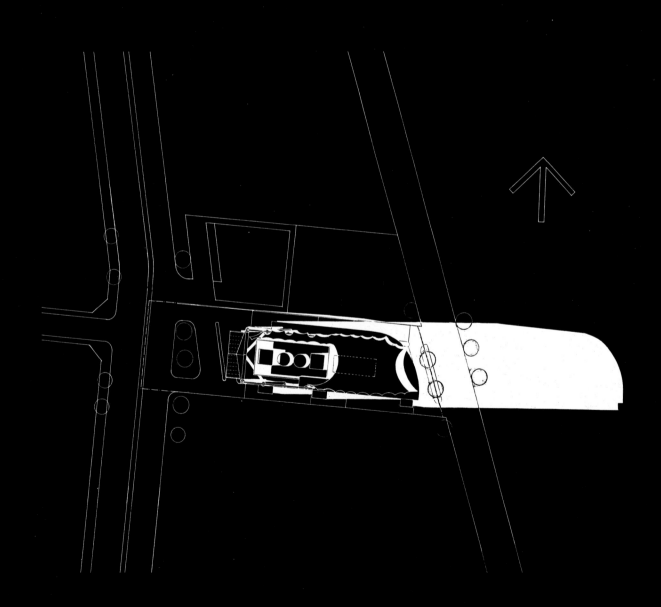

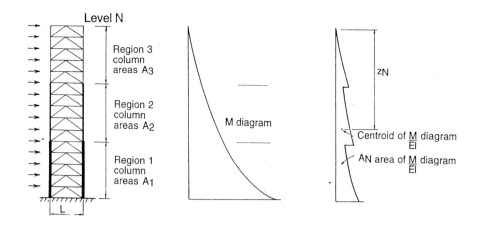

Level N

Region 3
column
areas A_3

Region 2
column
areas A_2

Region 1
column
areas A_1

L

M diagram

zN

Centroid of $\frac{M}{EI}$ diagram

AN area of $\frac{M}{EI}$ diagram

Development plan based on the
narrow initial prism.

Plan of the site.

Structural plan taking into account
the strong horizontal winds.

Ground floor at access level.

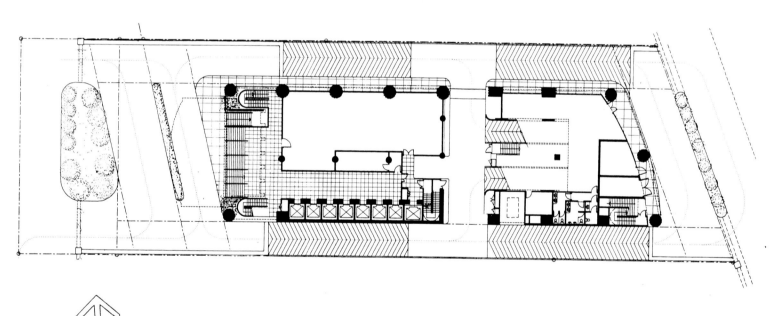

The service and communications nucleus on the south
side of the building serves as a kind of climatic
cushion, shielding the offices from the most intense
sunlight during the day, and providing natural light to
these service areas, which are normally found in the
center of buildings.

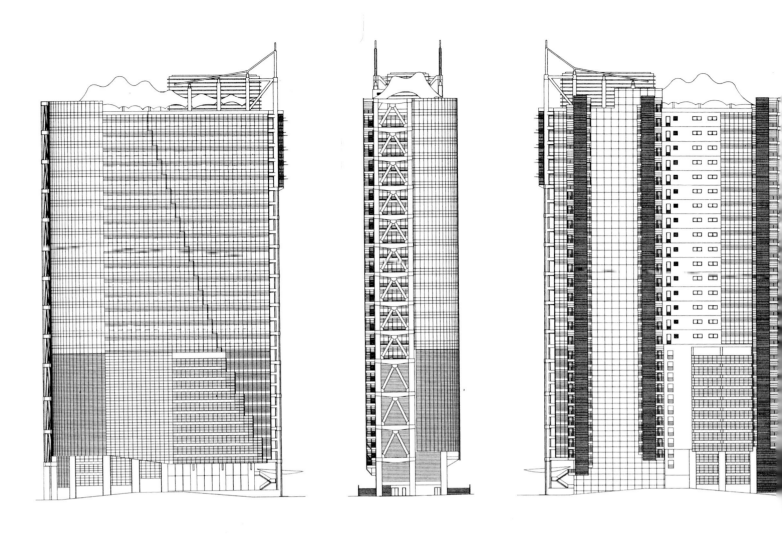

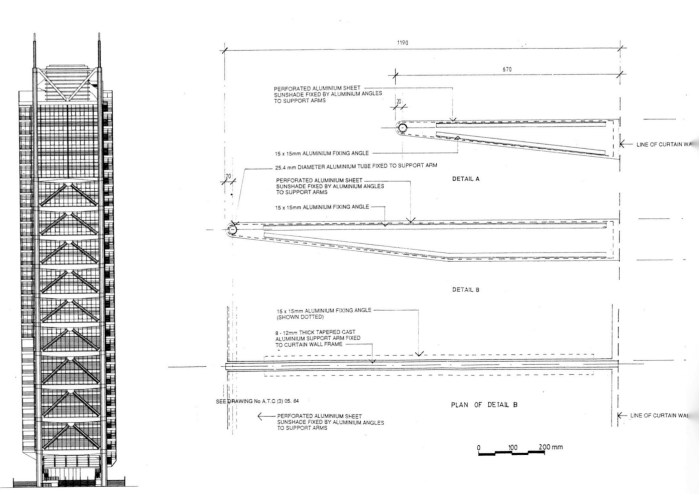

1190

670

PERFORATED ALUMINIUM SHEET
SUNSHADE FIXED BY ALUMINIUM ANGLES
TO SUPPORT ARMS

20

LINE OF CURTAIN WALL

15 x 15mm ALUMINIUM FIXING ANGLE

25.4 mm DIAMETER ALUMINIUM TUBE FIXED TO SUPPORT ARM

DETAIL A

20

PERFORATED ALUMINIUM SHEET
SUNSHADE FIXED BY ALUMINIUM ANGLES
TO SUPPORT ARMS

15 x 15mm ALUMINIUM FIXING ANGLE

DETAIL B

15 x 15mm ALUMINIUM FIXING ANGLE
(SHOWN DOTTED)

8 - 12mm THICK TAPERED CAST
ALUMINIUM SUPPORT ARM FIXED
TO CURTAIN WALL FRAME

SEE DRAWING No A.T.C (3) 05. 84

PLAN OF DETAIL B

PERFORATED ALUMINIUM SHEET
SUNSHADE FIXED BY ALUMINIUM ANGLES
TO SUPPORT ARMS

LINE OF CURTAIN WALL

0   100   200 mm

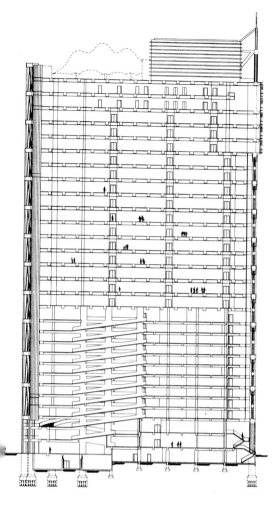

North face.

East face.

South face.

Longitudinal section. On the first floors, there are communication ramps between the different parking levels.

Views of the north and west faces. On the west side the structure is separated, throwing shadow over the wall.

West face.

Details of the structure of the metallic parasols on the west face.

Detail of the west face with the protecting parasols.

The terrace swimming pool with extensive views over the city.

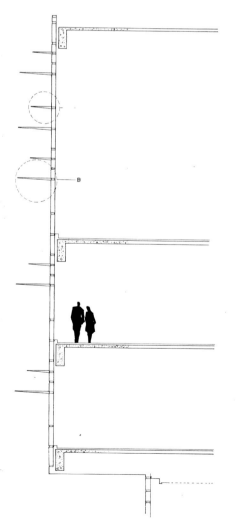

The 58,000 square meters of the building's total surface area, distributed over 27 stories, is organized according to a simple plan that stratifies uses by floors. The lower floors contain the lobbies, nuclei of vertical communications, and vehicle access to the parking elevators. The 334 parking spaces are on the first 11 floors, thus occupying almost a quarter of the total constructed space. The remaining floors, free of pillars—as required by the client—are dedicated to office space. The terraced roof contains, in addition to the escalator head, a sinuously shaped swimming pool with extensive views over the city and surrounding district.

Canopy roof of the lobby
entrance on the west side.

Access passages to the
service and communications
nucleus on the office floors.

Basic plan of office floor.
The communications and
service nucleus protects the
office space from the heat of
the south facade.

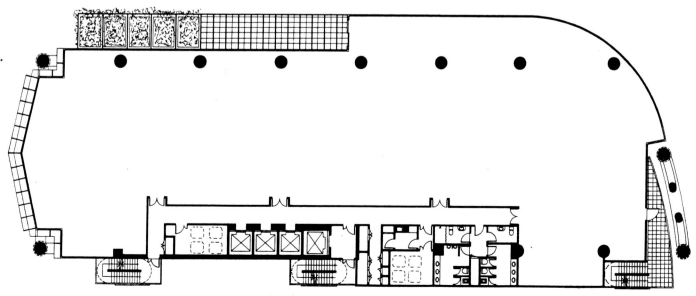

0   5   10 METRES

Access lobby on ground floor.

Canopy roof of the lobby entrance
on the west side.

Plaza Centenario

SAO PAULO, 1995

The Plaza Centenario carries to the limit the logic of spatial profitability—the yardstick by which this type of office block is judged. The decision of the architects was definitive and unwavering: free the floor space to the maximum, and concentrate all elements needed for structure and function in the skin of the tower. The building's final image corresponds to what i expected from such a building. The coldness of glass and aluminum is somehow satisfying, as i the use of these industrialized materials fulfills the mythified ideal of sophisticated, modern, technological construction.

The cornerstones of the architect's vision are constructive pragmatism and a strict adherence to the guidelines of the project. This thinking is reflected in the façade of the building. Continuou horizontal windows mark each floor, so that from the exterior the repetition of floors is clearly marked. The perimeter nuclei are opaque, with the folds of their concrete walls producing small vertical openings. These nuclei rise above the top floor of the building, emphasizing thei independence and supporting the installations terrace that includes a helicopter landing pad. The main entrance from Nações Unidas Avenue leads under the building's tribune, with its projecting canopy roof, and through the building to the main lobby. Here, the great structural walls are converted into four gigantic cylindrical pillars with a diameter of 2.5 meters, whose presence invades the space of the lobby. The tribune of the main façade has also been constructed with panes of glass that hide the carpentry underneath. The glass stops three meters from the ground, adding to its expressiveness and obliging visitors to enter under its protection, so that they perceive the mass of the building soaring above their heads.

Aerial view of the building.

The building has 32 stories above ground and six subterranean floors, amounting to a total of 77,500 square meters. The basic floor plan is a lesson in how to resolve a space intended for offices by providing a large, open area and avoiding conditioning it for its subsequent distribution into offices. To achieve this free space of 16 by 63 meters unobstructed by pillars or installations, the architect has placed the vertical communication nuclei in the center of the building, with two groups of six elevators symmetrically arranged on each side of the floor. The structure of the tower is also concentrated in the center of the building, with eight huge concrete walls and the elevator shafts supporting the panels, and four secondary service nuclei which allow its bracing at the extremes. In addition, a perimeter girder of 2.11 meters supports the transveral support girders on each floor, transmitting their load to the vertical nuclei, thus avoiding the need for pillars. The building is dressed with panels of silver Alucobond.

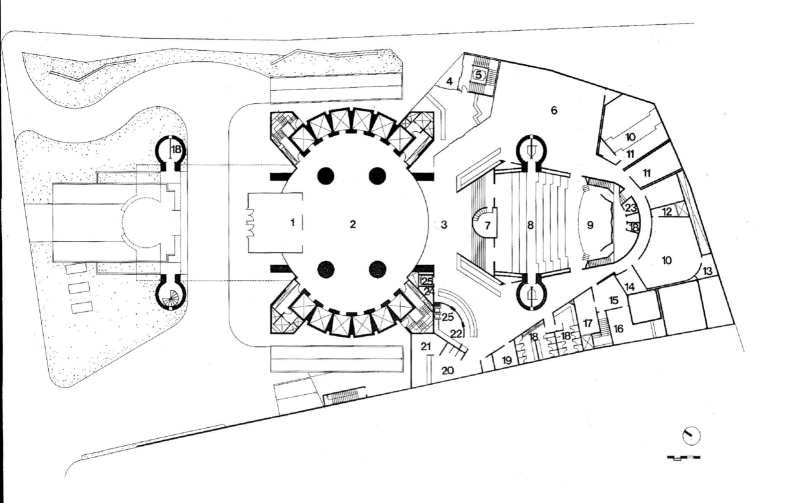

Ground floor.

1. Entrance.
2. Hall.
3. Foyer.
4. Entrance to the restaurant.
5. Lifts.
6. Exhibition room.
7. Projection booth.
8. Auditorium- Convention Hall.
9. Stage.
10. Smaller auditoriums.
11. Conference room.
12. Simultaneous translation booth.
13-25. Ancillary services rooms.

Standard floor plan. Fire regulations mean that the floor must be dividable into two independent sections.

1. Offices.
2. Hall.
3. Wash-rooms.
4. Emergency lift.
5. Corridor.
6. Air conditioning.

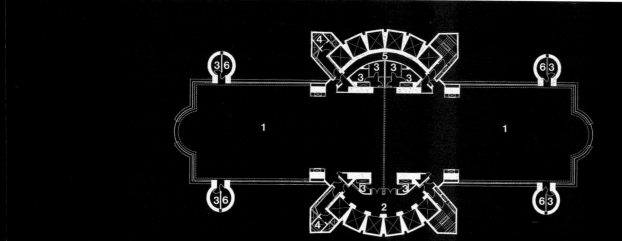

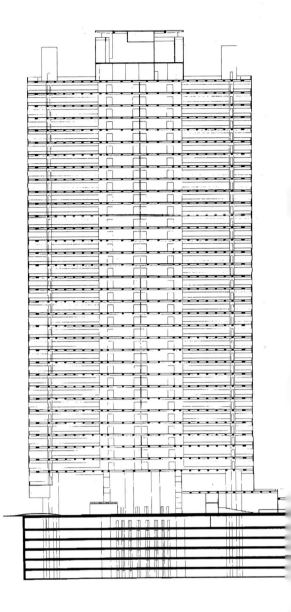

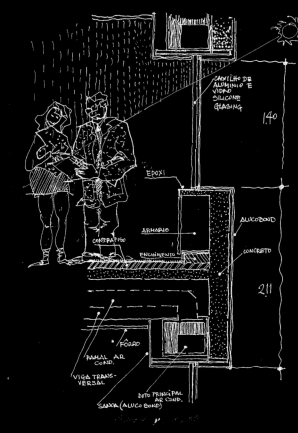

Section along the
longitudinal axis.

The Plaza Centenario stands out
from the other buildings due to
its height and finish.

Aerial view showing the contrast
between the horizontal bands
formed by the windows and the
vertical power of the nuclei.

Main façade seen from Avenida
Naçoes Unidas.

Drawing with detailed study of
the construction section

Different solutions for topping-off
the tribune of the main façade.

The glass tribune which stops before reaching the ground.

The lateral nuclei gather together and brace the floors of the tower.

The main entrance with access to the lobby covered by the spectacular projecting canopy.

KISHO KUROKAWA

Melbourne Central

MELBOURNE, 1991

This complex building is situated in the central business district of Melbourne. It includes offices, commercial and leisure areas, and even a metro station. Many activites and functions are juxtaposed in the space of this single complex. The architect has striven for heterogeneity both in the building's mass and in the appearance and the use of its materials. To create this varied architecture, fragments taken from the iconography of architecture and modern art are cited. Thus, the sphere, the cone, the inverted cone, cylinders, and parallelepipeds are all used.

Under an immense glass cone, the central space opens in the form of an atrium. This constitutes the real heart of the commercial center. Numerous balconies look out over it and facilitate the vertical movement of shoppers. In the center of the atrium is a pre-existing factory, which has been conserved not only because of its own architectural quality, but also because the citizens of Melbourne recognize it as something familiar.

In spite of the bluntness of its size and form, the office tower uses various mechanisms to meet the ground level, tempering the view of the building from the street. As in another design by the same author, the Central Plaza in Brisbane (1988), the prismatic volume of the tower seems to be converted, by means of small incisions, into a natural mineral crystal. Two the corners of the square-base prism are gradually chamfered, while the other two mitigate the arris effect through the quartering of the carpentry combined with aluminum sheeting. Other oblique cuts create gables in the roof. These mechanisms act on the prism to produce a lightness of effect as the eye ascends the tower.

The building has a surface area of more than 260,000 square meters, although the 26,000 square meter site does not occupy all of its block. On the west side the building is supported by the six floors of the commercial center, which appears as background to the imposing mass of the tower. On the east, where the entrance is placed, an immense roof with a tubular structure offers visitors a space of medium height that cushions the meeting between the public walkways and the lobby.

On the previous page.

The old tower of the factory and the exterior office tower compete under the cone, thanks to its transparency.

On this page.

Melbourne's business district, with the potent presence of the Melbourne Plaza tower.

View from the east. The silhouette of the commercial building softens the presence of the tower in the background.

The siting of the complex in
Melbourne's business district.

Entrance to the commercial center, showing the composition of the tower, the cone, the geodesic dome, and the diversity in the use of materials.

Aerial view of the atrium.

Balconies in the atrium.

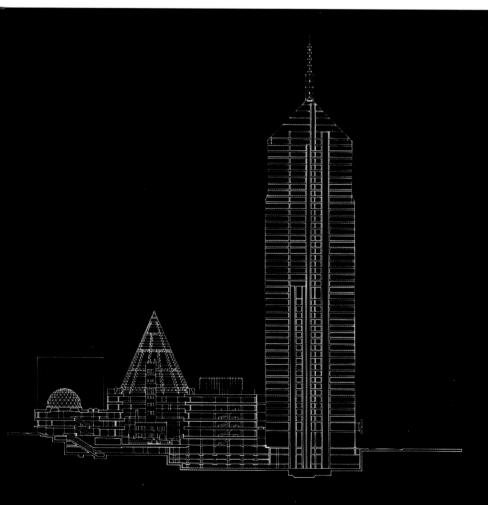

The old factory, under the cone, is the protagonist of the central area of the atrium.

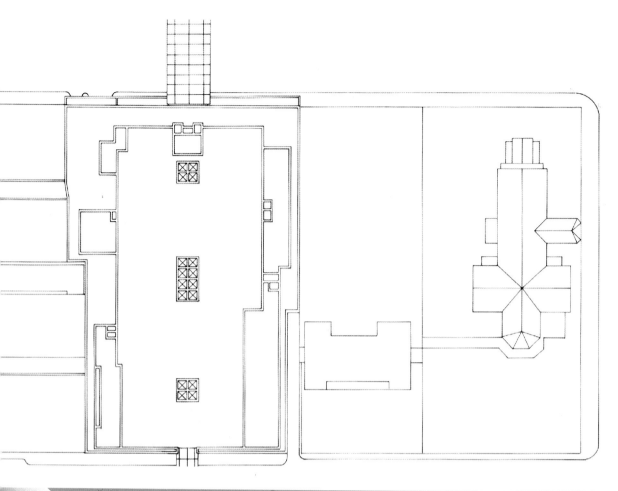

ADRIAN D. SMITH
SKIDMORE, OWINGS & MERRILL (SOM)

Jin Mao Building

SHANGHAI, 1998

Together with the two other projects in Shanghai presented in this book, the 21st Century Tower and the Shanghai World Financial Center, the Jin Mao Building may be seen as reflecting the rapid change that the economy of China is undergoing. The frenetic pace of real estate development is a product of the country's determination to become a first-division player among the world's economies. A longstanding notion is that the most impressive image of change and progress is the skyscraper. Height takes on a kind of symbolism and becomes an issue for competitiveness. China seems to have adopted this kind of thinking.

Still under construction, this 88-story building brings to mind the shape of Chinese pagodas, with its stepped height and the final crown. Working with vernacular forms has been one the continuing interests shown by Adrian D. Smith, a partner in the Chicago office of SOM, since he joined the firm in 1969, and in this project he relies on an image that lies deep in the collective consciousness of the country to integrate the tower into its urban context.

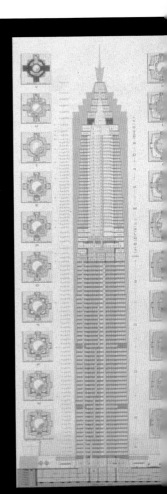

The tower is enclosed by gardens acting as an intermediate area with the surrounding streets. The building has entrances on all four sides, reinforcing a symmetry that is also found in the placement of the elevator shafts. The building's first 50 floors are allocated to office space, while the remaining 38, with their privileged view of the city, are occupied by a luxury hotel. This arrangement means that access to the busier areas of office space is simpler. On the fifty-sixth floor, a grand atrium begins and reaches to the top floor, providing an interesting configuration for the interior of the hotel.

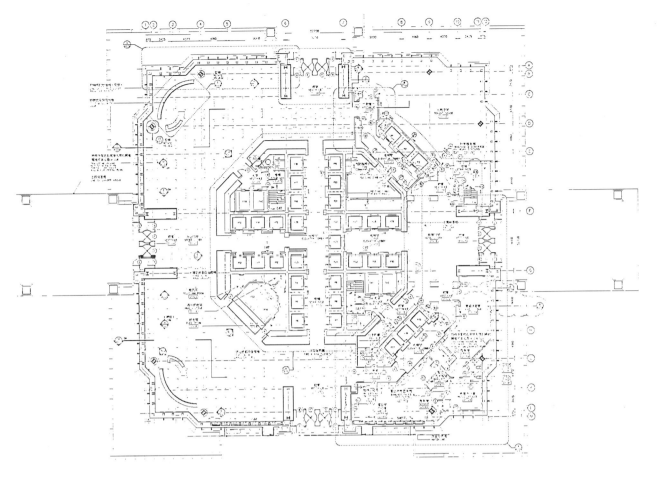

底层平面
A GROUND LEVEL PLAN

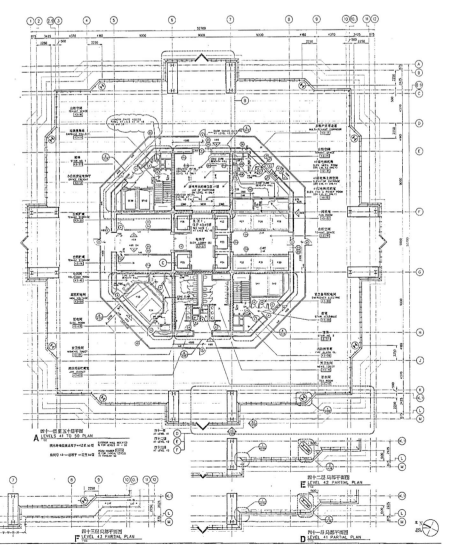

四十一层至五十层平面
A LEVELS 41 TO 50 PLAN

四十二层局部平面
E LEVEL 42 PARTIAL PLAN

四十三层局部平面
F LEVEL 43 PARTIAL PLAN

四十一层局部平面
D LEVEL 41 PARTIAL PLAN

Ground floor of the tower.

Floor plan of office floors.

Section. The great atrium of the hotel opens up from the 56th floor upwards.

A 1:1 scale model of the façade—a curtain wall of granite, aluminum and stainless steel—was constructed to conduct wind resistance tests.

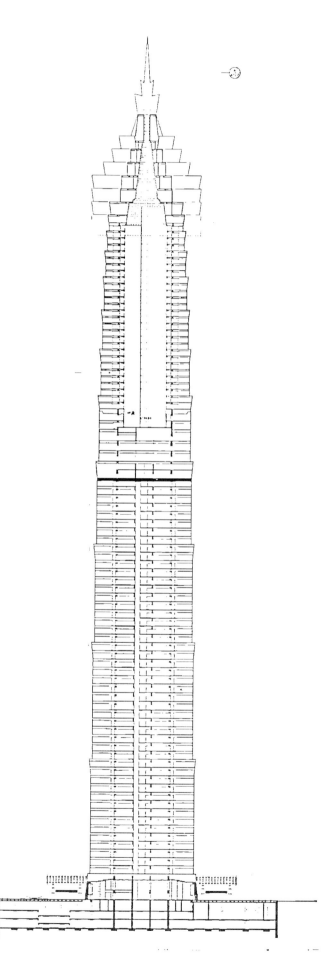

The structural and foundation systems were determined by geographical geological constraints, which had to take into account periodic earthquakes and typhoons. In addition, the site is on a river delta composed of sand and clay with no strata of harder rocks, even at the maximum level of 100 meters explored by the geotechnical prospecting team. Despite these problems, the building has three subterranean floors for car and bicycle parking. The building's foundation is a continuous slab with a depth of 4 meters and supported by 429 hollow steel piles descending for 65 meters. The building's main structure is composed of a central nucleus of concrete and eight slabbed pillars that form a continuous perimeter in order to absorb the horizontal force of typhoon winds. To free the interior of the building completely and facilitate distribution of office space, eight smaller pillars, placed between the larger ones, are also on the perimeter.

Shanghai World Financial Center

SHANGHAI, 1997–2001

The Shanghai World Financial Center, to be built in the financial and commercial district of Lujiazui, is planned to become an important landmark in the Pudong, an area on the opposite side of the river from the famous Bund. Shanghai is presently undergoing a period of sustained economic growth, and most hopes for the future are centered on Pudong, where the great majority of skyscrapers currently being planned for the 21st century will be situated.

The World Finance Center is still in the planning stage. Work is expected to begin in 1997, with the project being completed sometime in 2001. The plans for this 95-story skyscraper, 460 meters high with 300,000 square meters of floor space, include a hotel, shopping center, underground parking, and observation deck. The complex will be divided into two parts, the tower itself and a lower building. The tower will accommodate the hotel and the observation deck, while the other facilities are concentrated in the lower building, which will also serve as an intermediary structure between the tower and the ground.

The striking point about this project is not necessarily the design program itself, but rather the manifest wish on the part of its developers that the building become an unavoidable landmark in Shanghai's urban landscape. As a consequence of this wish, the aerodynamic tower will feature a great circular orifice in its upper floors, an interesting sharpness of its arrises, and a smooth skin which will reflect the changes in light throughout the day.

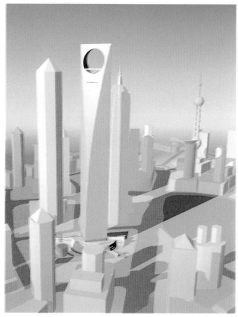

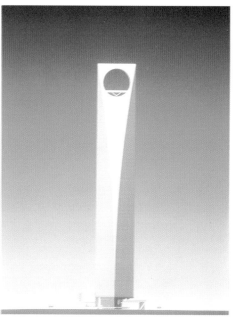

Longitudinal section and site plan.

Various computer generated views of the
project and its integration with the urban
context of Shangha.

21st Century Tower

SHANGHAI, 1994

The 21st Century Tower, still under development, is situated in the financial area of Lujiazui, which lies within the new expanded urban district of Pudong. The modestly-sized site occupies a privileged position within the area, facing the famous Shanghai Bund, the prototypical district of the city's central area. The Tower can perhaps best be understood as an icon in the city, an easily recognizable and representative image for the Pudong area.

The complex is composed of two differentiated parts: the 49-story tower, and a low three-story building at its base which serves as a kind of podium. The supporting structure of the building is on its exterior and is painted red for expressiveness. This structure is modified in the northeast corner by the elimination of the column of the vertex in the first nine floors, thus softening the building's meeting with the ground and heightening the visual access to it.

This structural gesture emphasizes an essential element of the project: the so-called Sky Gardens. These meeting areas—nine-story-high empty spaces within the tower—are distinguished by the use of plain glass, whereas in the rest of the building blue or green glass is used in order to highlight the red-painted structure of the tower. The idea of a mass of empty space within a rectangular skyscraper will be used by Murphy and Jahn in subsequent designs in order to realize the expressive and bioclimatic opportunities offered by this kind of juxtaposition.

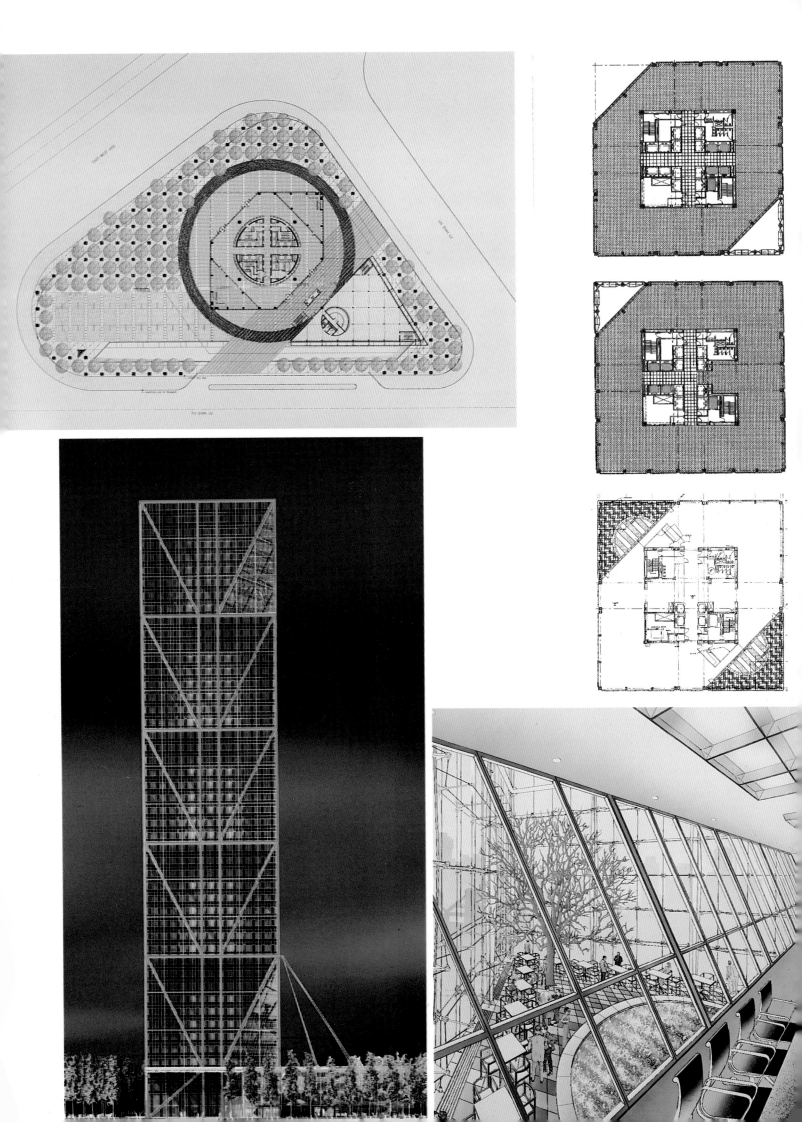

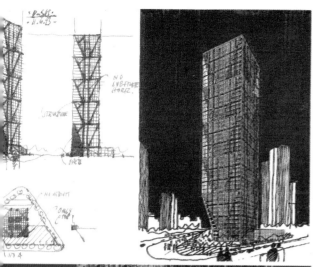

Site plan.

Fifth floor.

Basic floor plan. The shape of
the northeast corner varies at
different levels in accord with
the volume of the *Skygarden*.

The forty-first floor is
unique in having *Skygardens*
in two of its corners.

View of one of the
Skygardens from the
interior of the building.

The Endless Towers and Brancusi Tower

SINGAPORE, 1995

The Endless Towers and the Brancusi Tower have their origen in the 21st Century Tower project in Shanghai, also by the firm of Murphy/Jahn, and have evolved from typological concepts expressed in the Shanghai project. These include the perforation of the mass of the prism by the inclusion of so-called Skygardens, voids several stories high within the building which are used for relaxation and to perform a role in the climatic control of the building.

The Brancusi Tower has been conceived as a completely theoretical exercise—the exploration of an idea in its purest form—and as such is not restrained by practical or economic questions. The shape for the design is taken from the sculpture created by Brancusi in 1918, titled Endless Column.

The Endless Towers, on the other hand, are actually planned to be constructed in Singapore. The Skygardens, situated in the four corners of the towers play a vital role in controlling the climate of the buildings. Air expelled from the offices is warmed by direct sunlight, and since it is lighter, it rises, diminishing the humidity in the atmosphere and finally escaping through the roof of the building. Visually, the Skygardens have the effect of making the limits of the buildings much less precise, thereby creating a completely different image.

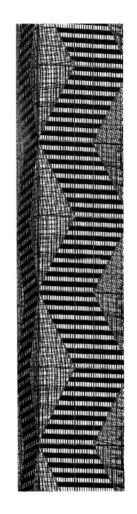

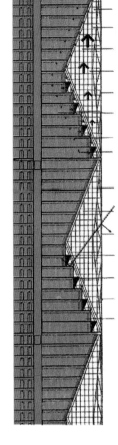

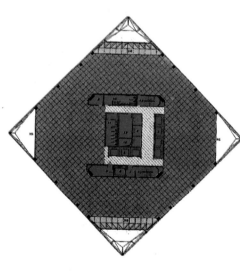

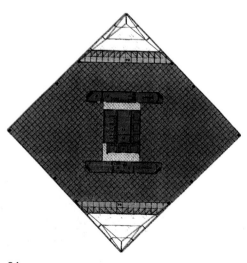

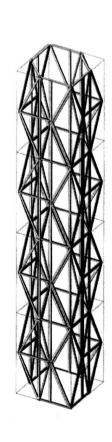

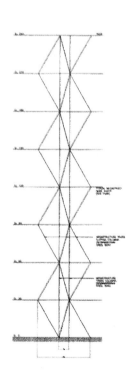

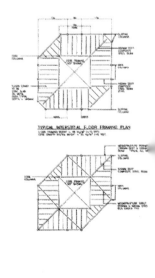

TYPICAL INTERSTITIAL FLOOR FRAMING PLAN

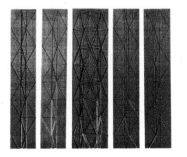

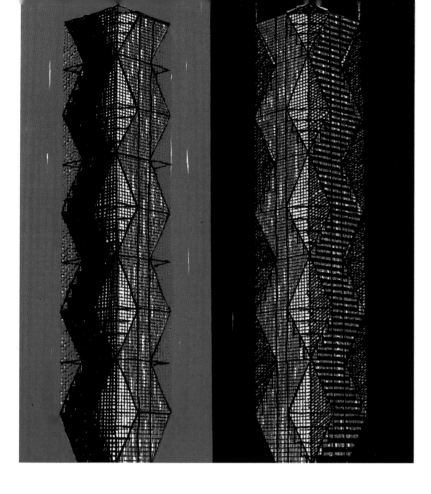

Sketches for the Brancusi Tower showing how the volumetry, perforated by the Skygardens, is the essential force of the project. The outer arrises of the tower become broken lines which completely change the idea of how skyscrapers look.

The model for the Skygardens.

Face and section.

Floor plans, which vary from level to level due to the variable configuration of the Skygardens.

Structural analysis of the building.

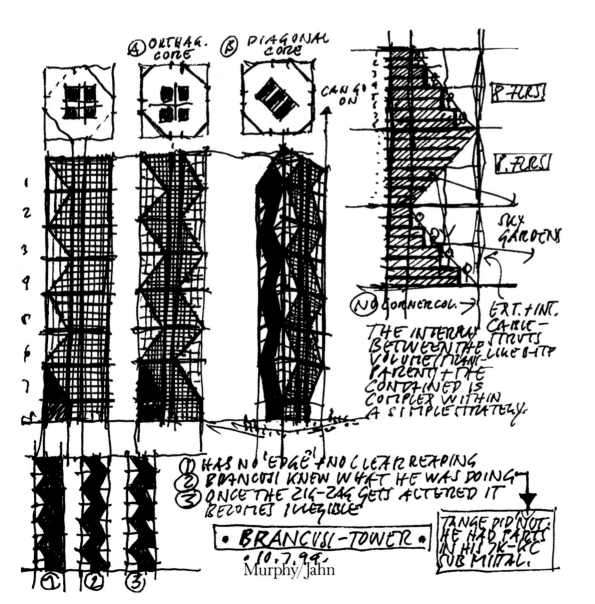

Generale Bank Tower

ROTTERDAM

The General Bank Tower occupies a corner bordered by the Blaak Canal and the Schielandhuis in Rotterdam's Blaak office area. The site is complicated from the point of view of urban planning due its strategic position at the intersection of two of the busiest streets in the area and because of the need to establish relationships with the buildings that surround it. Given this mature urban environment, Murphy/Jahn decided to respond with partial solutions offered by the immediate surroundings, and then to unify these solutions afterward. The key to this strategy was the uniform treatment of the façades with continuity in the use of finishing materials.

The first important decision was to concentrate the mass of the General Bank Tower itself at the edge of the site, in the angle formed by the canal and the street, thus freeing the rest of the ground to be occupied by a public square in front of the Maritime Museum. This curve is the most characteristic image of the tower, and is achieved by making nearly all the façade, from the fourth floor to the top, project out over space. The view of the General Bank Tower from the city is of an entirely different nature. Here, what is seen is a massive rectangle with angular corners. This is expressed by a prominent mass contrasting with the curved glass tribune supporting it. Instead of the expressive verticality of the overhang, the view from the city is of the horizontality of the parapets interrupting the continuity of the pillars.

In an attempt to minimize the effect of the building's crown over the neighboring housing block, the façade facing Blaak Canal is lightened. This process is continued on the lateral side, where the building descends in steps toward Korte Hoogstraat, allowing sunlight to reflect off its arrises and be captured by the nearby façades and the public plaza.

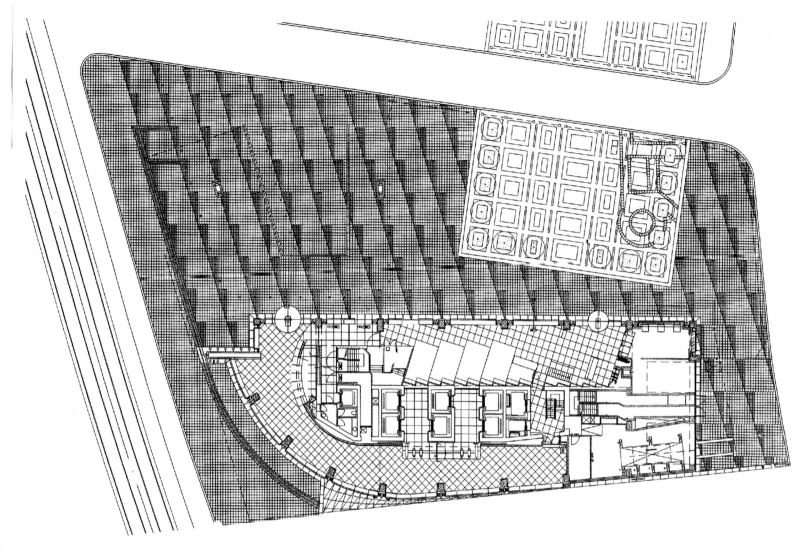

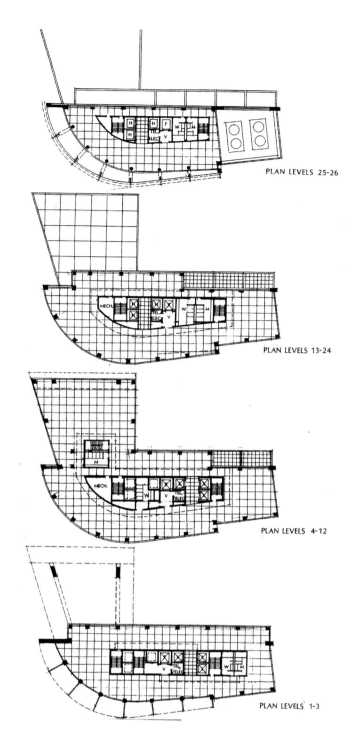

PLAN LEVELS 25-26

PLAN LEVELS 13-24

PLAN LEVELS 4-12

PLAN LEVELS 1-3

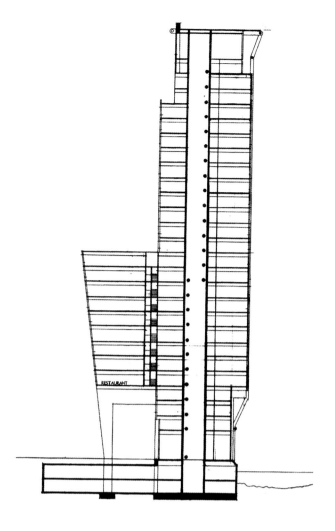

RESTAURANT

Ground floor of the Tower, with the design in the pavement and the enlargement of the Maritime Museum garden.

The volume of the building is raised to allow it to connect with the plaza and the Maritime Museum.

Typical floor plans and section of the General Bank Tower.

Foreshortened view of the building from the Schielandhuis, showing the inclination of the façade at the entrance to Korte Hoogstraat.

Architect's drawings exploring
various possibilities.

The interior of the General Bank Tower is based on a module of 1.8 meters, which is used to give modular spaces between 5.4 and 7.2 meters in width, normal dimensions for leased office space. This modulation is the basis of the structure: the pillars are placed every four modules, and the external windows and the finishes of the floors and ceilings are also adapted around this basic plan. In addition, the siting of the service and communications nuclei in the center of the tower, and the placement of the pillars in the exterior skin of the building, mean that the internal space can be divided up with complete freedom, thus increasing the marketability of the space.

The Korte Hoogstrat façade
showing the upper void and the
rotation of the superior part of
the pergola, seeking to reconcile
the different faces.

View from Blaak Canal showing
the massive block and the
projecting tribune which it
supports, and the recessed façade.

DG Bank Frankfurt

FRANKFURT, 1993

The design program for the DG Bank in Frankfurt was complex, as it was proposed that the building include leased office space, a hotel, apartments, restaurants, and commercial space, as well as the offices intended for the bank itself. The building is located in the central Bahnhoff district near the old part of the city, and overlooks the commercially important Mainzer Landstrasse. The project includes not only the tower but also lower buildings. The project therefore abandons the classical skyscraper composition of a single, monolithic structure, and tries to respond honestly to the complexity and heterogeneity of this specific part of the city.

This response to the urban context is shown not only in the volumetric distribution of the complex, but also in the varied mixture of uses tailored to the needs of the zone. While the tower is used exclusively for office space, the lower buildings are home to a range of uses that bring the project closer to the needs of the citizens of Frankfurt. The complicated emplacement of the site, forming part of a new concentration of high-rise blocks in a quiet residential district near the rail station, proved to be significant in the development of the project.

Plan of the site's emplacement in the residential district near Frankfurt station.

View of Mainzer Landstrasse. The crowning diadem is a distinctive identifying sign of the tower in the Frankfurt skyline.

The volumes of the complex vary in height in answer to the specific problems posed by the surroundings on each side of the site. The tower rises up from among the buildings that face the main street, while the other, lower, L-shaped volumes surrounding the tower act as intermediaries between the tower and neighboring buildings. A large, completely symmetrical entrance hall in the middle of the buildings gives access not only to the office space in the tower, but also to the public spaces on the lower floors, which include shops, restaurants, and cafés. The building's crowning glory is a giant diadem that has become the identifying symbol of the complex.

94

The complex has a total surface area of 77,000 square meters, centering on the 208-meter tower, the highest building in Frankfurt. The contemplated hotel was finally not included due to its probable lack of profitability, and the section of the building that was to be devoted to the hotel is now occupied by leased office space. However, the area intended for housing, and required by urban planning regulations, has been built. An area of about 1200 square meters of apartments occupies part of the northern part of the complex.

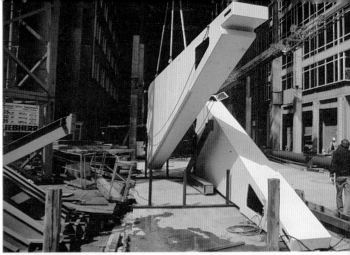

Axonometric perspectives.

Pieces of the crown of the tower before being lifted into place.

The large cornice, in addition to improving the look of the building, serves to hide the machinery needed for building services.

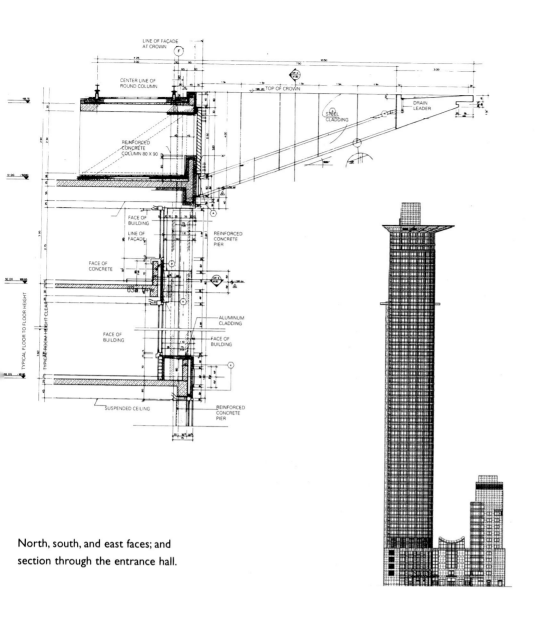

LINE OF FAÇADE
AT CROWN

CENTER LINE OF
ROUND COLUMN

TOP OF CROWN

STEEL
CLADDING

DRAIN
LEADER

REINFORCED
CONCRETE
COLUMN 80 X 90

FACE OF
BUILDING

LINE OF
FAÇADE

REINFORCED
CONCRETE
PIER

FACE OF
CONCRETE

ALUMINUM
CLADDING

FACE OF
BUILDING

FACE OF
BUILDING

SUSPENDED CEILING

REINFORCED
CONCRETE
PIER

TYPICAL FLOOR TO FLOOR HEIGHT
TYPICAL ROOM HEIGHT CLEAR

North, south, and east faces; and
section through the entrance hall.

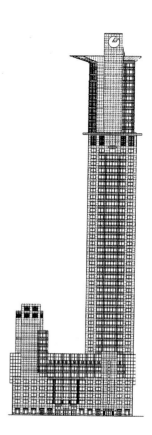

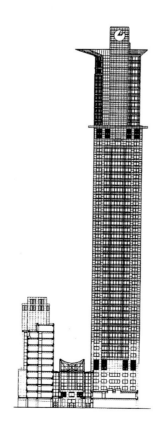

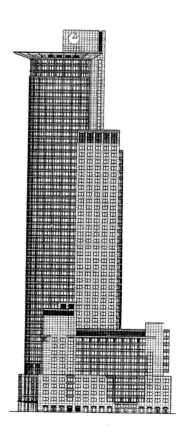

Entrance to the conservatory-
hall from Mainzer Landstrasse.

The conservatory-type entrance
hall offers a range of public
services.

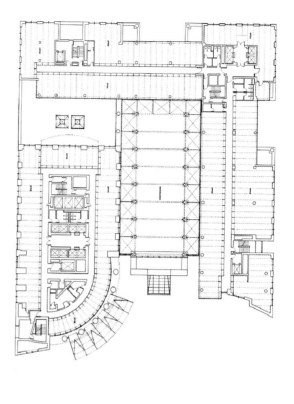

Plans of the different levels.

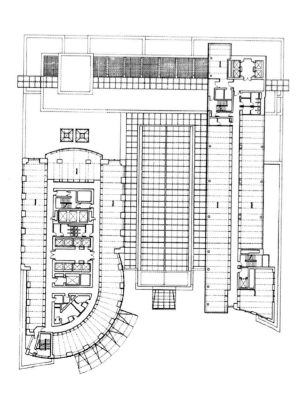

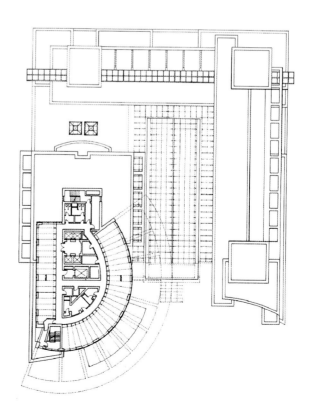

NTT Headquarters

TOKYO, 1990–1995

The headquarters of NTT is situated in the central district of Shinjuku, between the Tokyo City Hall and the new Opera House. It is comprised of three well-defined parts—a 30-story tower, a lower body, and a connecting garden. It was conceived as forming an integrated part of Tokyo's Shinjuku, one of the most important commercial, corporative, and cultural centers in Japan.

The site chosen by NTT for its headquarters was a rectangle severely constrained by its location at the intersection of two major thoroughfares and by the urban planning regulations affecting it. One side of the site is very close to Chuo Kosokudoro, a heavily used elevated motorway. Another impediment was the presence of electric cables which pass over the site and cannot be built over. The regulations governing the access of light stated that the shadow of the building should not fall on any adjacent construction for more than three hours a day and that the maximum height should be no more than 127 meters. In addition, an emergency landing for helicopters was required for the top of building, as the site lies in

a helicopter flight path. Finally, City Hall demanded the cession of 20% of the site for public space.

On the original rectangle, the architects drew the maximum possible envelopment of the building, drawn back from the limits of the site and with the arrises symmetrically rounded on the side touching the motorway. Once the envelopment had been determined, the architects divided the project into two buildings whose exterior façades follow the edge of this line—a slim tower united by its base to the parking area, and a low construction in the rounded area next to the elevated motorway. An interruption in the perimeter allows the intermediate space used as a public garden to be seen from Yamanote Dori street.

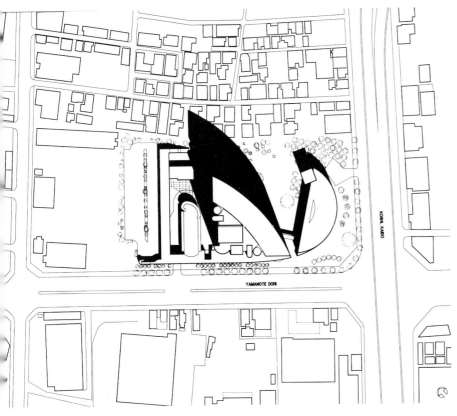

Plan of the site with a study
of the shadow effect.

The interruption of the
envelopment and the garden
access from Yamanote Dori.

The tower has 30 floors above ground for office use and another 6 floors below ground used for the telecommunications center, a conference room, and staff restaurant. It is divided into two well-defined parts, a curved band overlooking the interior garden which houses offices and a triangular area with an exterior façade dedicated to the services and communications areas. The four metallic sunshades on each floor modulate and reinforce this image of a stressed and unfinished façade, and allow a panoramic view from the offices with no obstruction from curtains or blinds.

The elevation from the
parking area.

The elevation from
Yamanote Dori.

The elevation from the Chuo
Kosokodoro motorway.

View from the residential
area sited to the north
of the complex.

The NTT building with the
Chuo Kosokodoro motorway
in the foreground.

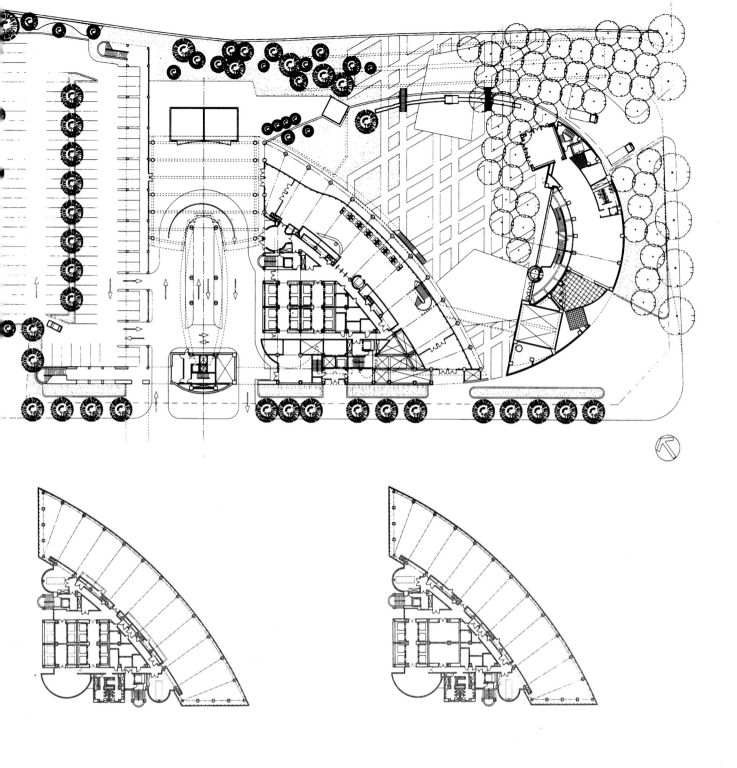

The interplay of lights and
shadows on the lateral façades.

Ground floor of the project.

Basic floor plans of the tower.

View of the
garden which
narrows toward
Yamanote Dori.

Access lobby on
the ground floor of
the tower, with a
view of the garden.

The linear pond lying at the upper limit of the garden.

Metallic stairs hanging over the three-floor high open space of the commercial center, with its façade onto the interior garden.

OUB Center

SINGAPORE, 1986

The Overseas Union Bank, one of the four largest banks in Singapore, faces Raffles Place in the center of the financial district. Its height of 280 meters makes it the tallest bank headquarters in Asia. During the redevelopment of this area of the city, the site of the bank was put aside and later auctioned publicly. This was partly because the site was conditioned by the building of the new central terminal of the MRT (underground railway) under Raffles Place itself. The space over the new station was used for the entrances and for a new public park. The view of the financial district as a whole, especially when seen from the other side of the Singapore River, leaves the OUB Center somewhat hidden by the buildings which surround it. To compensate for this slightly disadvantaged position, the building presents the continuity and flatness of its largest façade on this side. The result is a building that succeeds in distinguishing itself and standing out from the cluster of buildings surrounding it.

A joint breaks the building into two visually distinct parts. The joint between the building's two triangles runs the length of their intersection, and serves to perfectly delineate the two bodies. This recourse to formalism helps solve the problem of the interruption of the lower portion of building by marking its independence, and allows the façade of the higher tower to continue rising tranquilly above it. It comes as a surprise that this division of volume is not reflected in the interior of the building. The office space appears as an unbroken rectangle, with two perimetral service pockets in the floor plan to hide the indentation due to the joint.

The base of the building is formed by a low block which extends along one whole side of Raffles Place until it reaches the metropolitan rail station. A pedestrian bridge connects the atrium of this building with a public parking facility with a capacity for 3,000 cars. This, together with the rail station, ensures that access to the building is not a problem. The part of this base whose front faces Raffles Place is used as a shopping center, while the part opening onto the river avenue houses the entrances to the offices and to the OUB itself. The interior of the shopping center is characterized by a large open patio with triangular skylights that allow light to filter through in a manner reminiscent of the traditional blinds of worked wood found in older houses in Singapore.

View from the far bank of the
Singapore River, with the
buildings of the financial
center in profile.

110

Perspective from the
avenue which follows
the river bank, where
the prominent arris
which defines the
building confronts
the street axis.

The main entrance
to the tower, with the
offices used as
the Bank's headquarters
dominating the avenue.

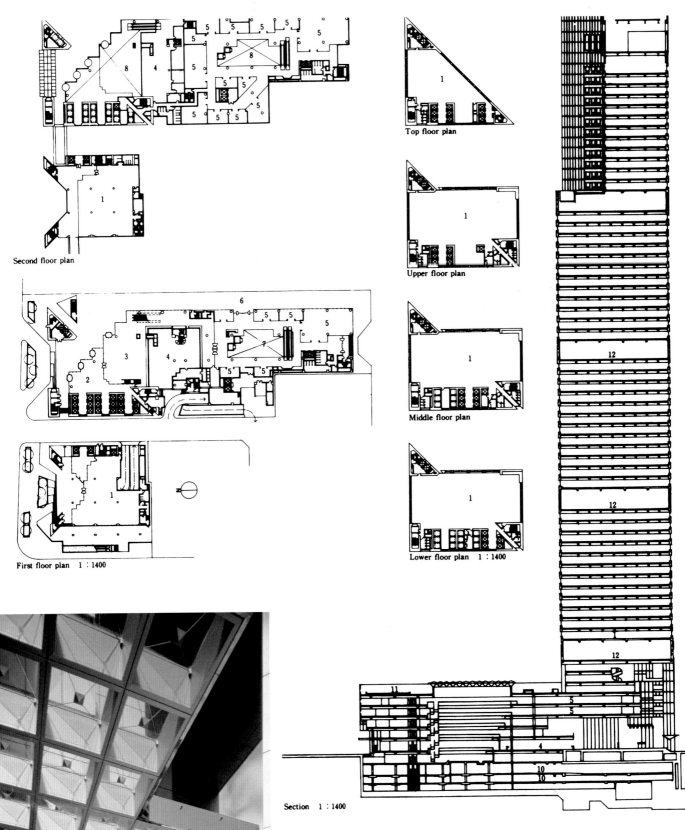

Second floor plan

First floor plan   1 : 1400

Top floor plan

Upper floor plan

Middle floor plan

Lower floor plan   1 : 1400

Section   1 : 1400

Floor plans and sections of the project.

The entrance to the offices covered by the large pergola, seen from Raffles Place.

Interior of the Bank's access lobby.

Citibank Plaza

HONG KONG, 1989-1992

Known as plot 8888, the land chosen by Citibank as the site of its new headquarters was the largest and best building site available in central Hong Kong. Located on the sea front between the old commercial area of Queen's Road Central and the new areas of Admiralty and Queensway, the plot is surrounded by some of the most important and representative buildings of city, including the the Bond Center and the Hong Kong Bank.

Opposite the new Citibank Plaza building stands the Bank of China, designed by the Chinese-American architect I.M. Pei. It has become one of the most emblematic constructions in the city. The Citibank building attempts to be sensitive to the imposing presence of the Bank of China, avoiding any form of direct confrontation esthetically, instead trying to provide a contrast of opposites. The decision was made to distance the building from its famous neighbor, placing the mass of the building on the furthest edge of the site, and creating a southern-oriented plaza between it and the Bank of China.

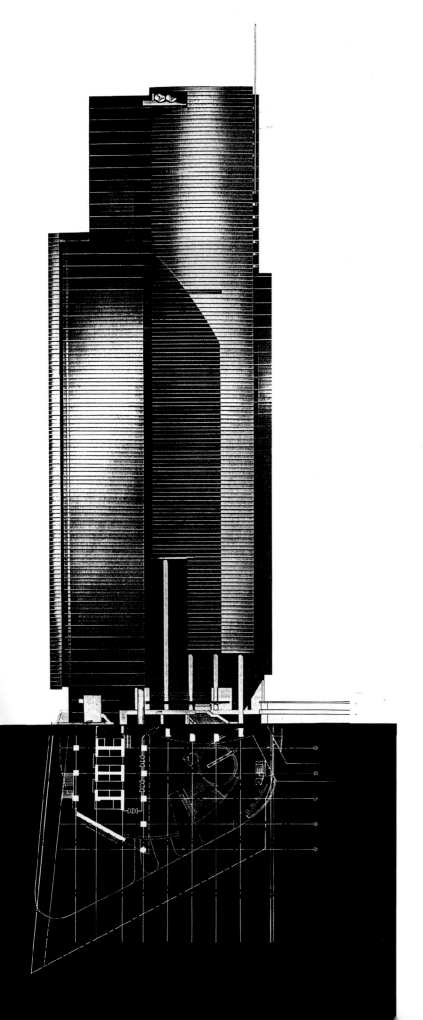

A second decision was to fragment the mass of the Citibank complex by splitting it into two towers of differing heights (50 and 40 floors), in order to provide a visual contrast to the monolithic nature of Pei's building. The façades of the towers are presented as stiff boards, denying any continuity to the corners by juxtaposing the flat and curved surfaces, and by leaving a shadowy chasm where the two towers meet. This contrasts with the smooth rotundity of the Bank of China façades and also with the articulation of the faces of the Bank of China building with massive angles.

Main elevation with the two towers of differing heights.

View from Queensway with I.M. Pei's skyscraper in the foreground.

The chasm running across the
two towers widens to
accommodate the entrance
between the two pillars.

Plan of the site.

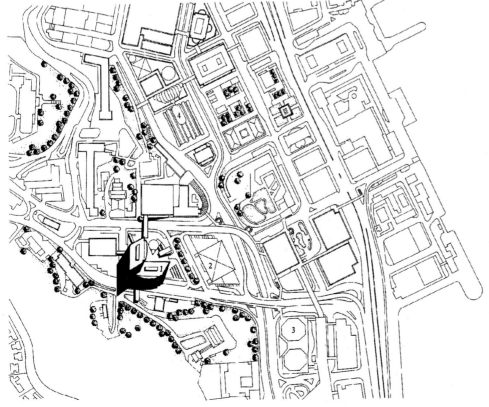

View from below of the pedestrian walkway that crosses the atrium in the entrance area.

Access walkway between the two communications nuclei on the lower levels.

Pedestrian entrance from Queen's Road Central.

The façade of the Citibank building stops before reaching the ground, leaving the supporting pillars exposed. The pillars are lightened by giving them a rounded form. They are stylized by fluting the columns and dressing them with natural aluminum. Together, they form an authentic colonnade around the plaza, helping to define the public space. From the plaza, the main entrance to the bank appears almost as if it were an excavation in the mass of the tower, tearing the skin of the lateral façades, prolonging the chasm that separates them and creating a 10-story-high atrium that assures the continuity of the plaza in the interior of the bank. This is part of what the architect has called "constructive synthesis," in which a collage of apparently unstable and incomplete parts interact amongst themselves to compose a dynamic whole—a visual metaphor of the spontaneity and energy of Hong Kong today.

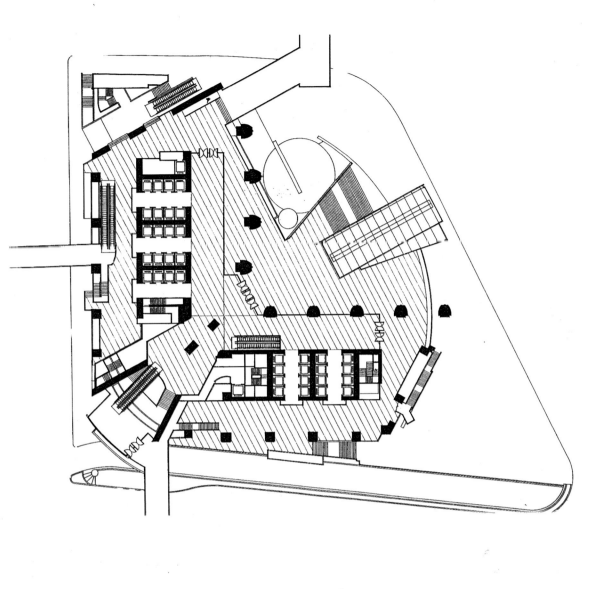

Entrance floor.

Upper platform.

Floor plan at street level.

Basic floor plan.

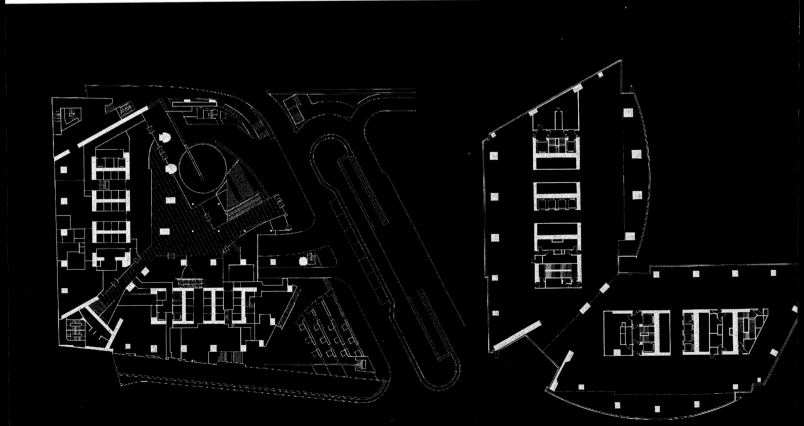

Interior stairs between the entrance area at street level and the elevated plaza.

Elevator lobby at the plaza level.

Detail of the change of stair rail between the ground floor and the pedestrian level of the plaza.

Suntec City

SINGAPORE, 1997

Singapore has changed from a medium-sized city with a strong colonial tradition into a metropolis competing internationally at the highest levels. Over the last few decades this city-state has become one of the world's most prosperous countries. However, such economic expansion has been carried out by means of a fierce capitalism that has left its mark, especially in the central business district, an area of high towers where the human scale has been forgotten. In this context, the team of Tsao & McKown have made a true effort in the design of Suntec City to create a civic space where the pedestrian still has a place in surroundings marked by great heights.

The site is located at the confluence of major city streets with the principal exits from the city, and has undergone various modifications in the street structure in order to improve connection with the old part of the city on the other side of the river. Between Suntec City and the old city, a green area flanking the river has been transformed into a public area on a scale matching that of the city, thus facilitating the posterior link between the two areas.

The scale of intervention in what is presently the largest private development in the country responds on one hand to the urban context of the surrounding towers, but on the other hand, pays special attention to the pedestrian.

The high and low towers and the convention center are
linked by a public area where the pedestrian can pass
by shops and restaurants near the convention center,
and come and go from the towers under the shadow of
the trees. This project represents a step forward in
comparison to its neighbors, and has become a symbol
for the people of Singapore, serving as a real civic
center which, in addition to providing a series of
services, is capable of attracting casual passersby who
can feel that they are protagonists of a space
constructed with them in mind.

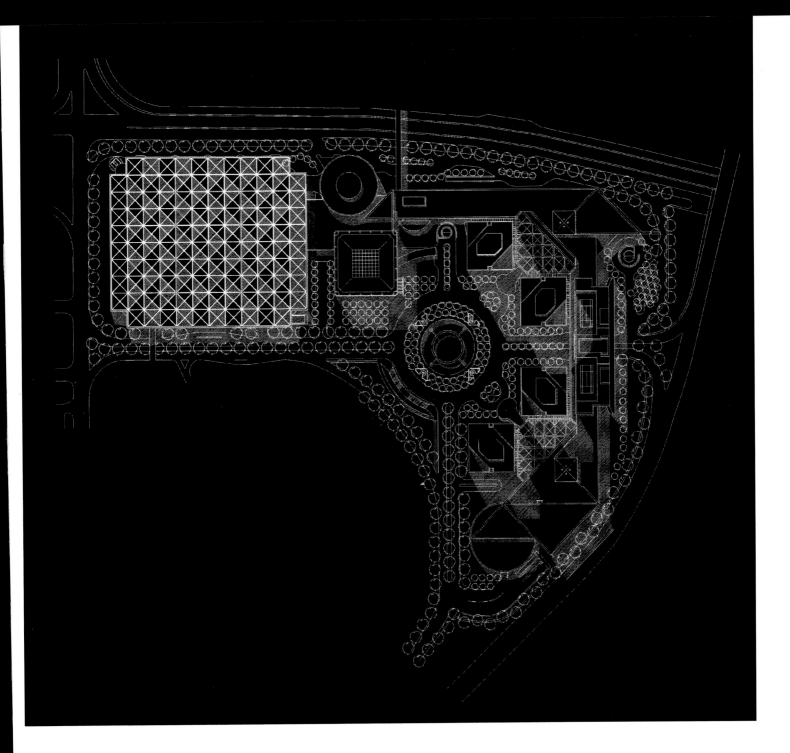

View of the urban context of the project, seen from the historical center of Singapore.

View of the roofs. The complex has a three-dimensional shape in the form of a hand.

Longitudinal section of the complex through the center of the plaza.

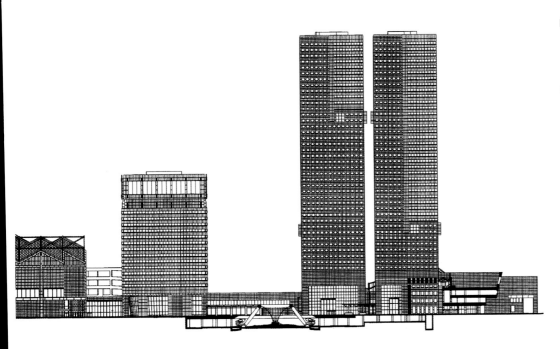

With a total surface area of 11.7 hectares, or more than 5 million square feet, Suntec City has four towers of offices, each with 45 floors, as well as a lower tower of 18 floors, a convention center, shops, cafeterias, and restaurants and spaces for leisure activities. All this is based on an L-shaped base which supports a three-dimensional shape in the form of a hand. The complex is articulated by the large central plaza, forming the palm of the hand, and serves as a type of "waiting room." Special attention has been paid here both to the climatic comfort of the area and to the visual sensations offered to pedestrians. A huge fountain in the shape of a metallic ring enhances the atmosphere.

View from one of the important avenues that define the project. The context is of tall office blocks.

The incursions into the volume at the feet of the towers give oblique views of the complex.

View over the three-dimensional roof of the convention center.

The fountain establishes a nexus between the two levels of the plaza.

Acacia trees create a shaded area, which, as the years pass, will form a dense, interwoven canopy, softening the visual encounter with the imposing towers. A network of metal pieces unites all the components of the complex, covering both the structure and the façade, such as the enormous roof of the convention hall. The finish is of the Univers system, which by its flexibility is able to solve all the problems posed by the multiple details and meeting points of the finish, and which facilitates construction in a project of this magnitude by using standard parts prefabricated in great quantities.

The incursions into the volume at the feet of the towers give new and unexpected views of the complex.

The lower tower serves as a link between the low mass of the convention center and the high towers.

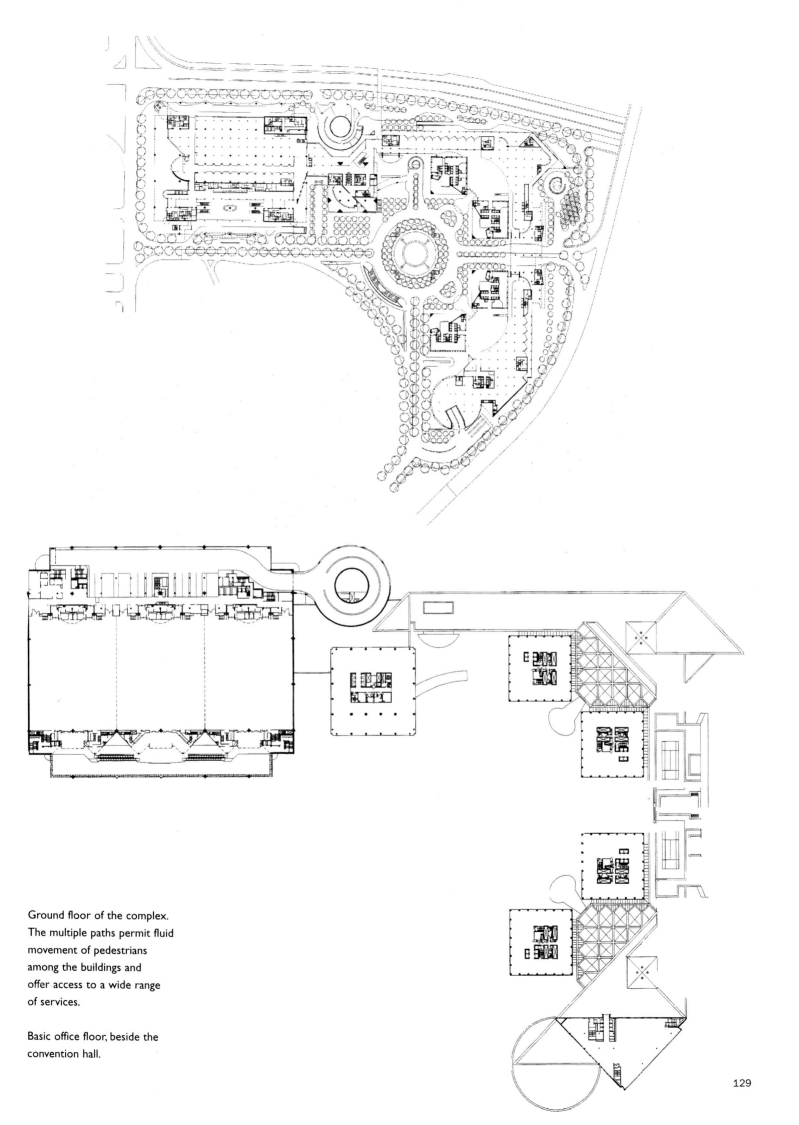

Ground floor of the complex.
The multiple paths permit fluid
movement of pedestrians
among the buildings and
offer access to a wide range
of services.

Basic office floor, beside the
convention hall.

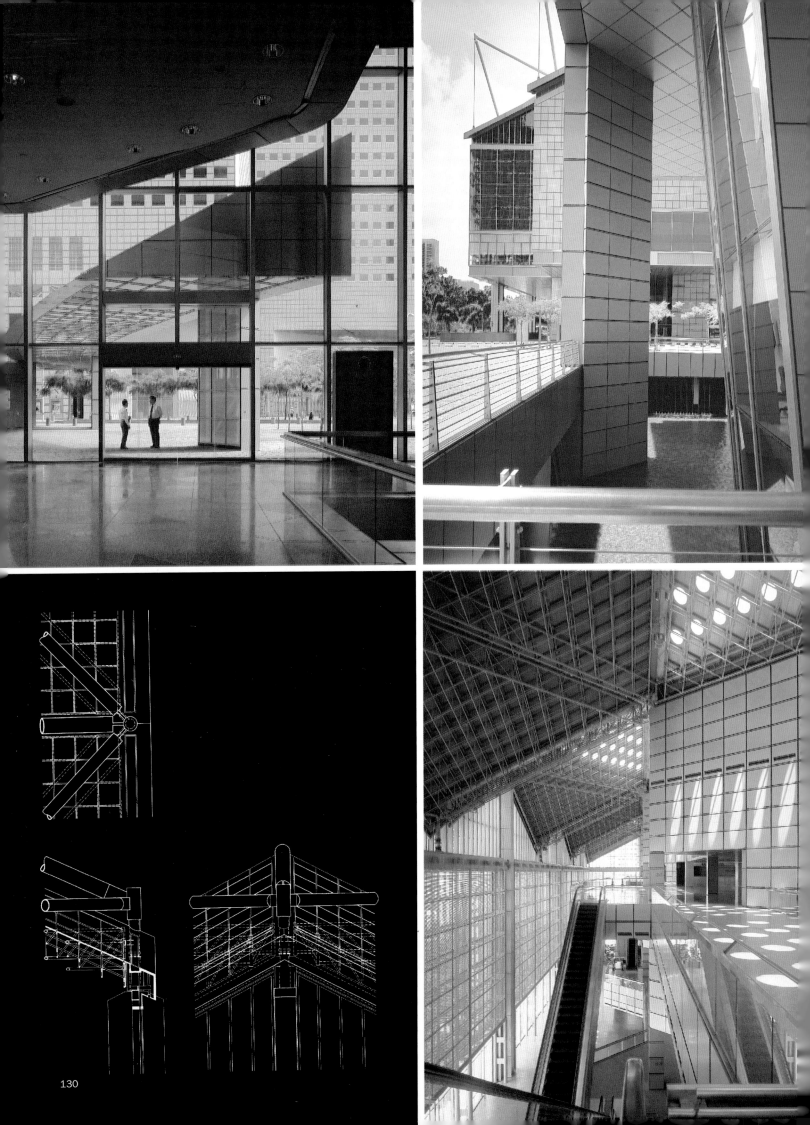

The transparency of the lobbies of the towers allows visual connection with the exterior of the plaza.

In front of the lower tower, the plaza disappears and the building seems to float on the water.

Details of the three dimensional tubular structure of the roof of the convention center where it meets the façade.

Interior of the convention center, which also has commercial space.

Entrance to the three-story commercial area that unites the complex.

French National Library

PARIS, 1996

The French National Library is the last great work conceived under the mandate of the former President of the Republic, François Mitterand. Its main characteristics are simplicity and the integration of volumes. Four glass towers, with shelves for books, define the squares of an immense rectangular podium and enclose a large open space. Besides being the number of towers in the project, four is also the number of materials are used throughout the project—glass, wood, steel and concrete.

The recurring use of the same materials is marked by a rare sensitivity, free from any wish for ornamentation. Each part of the building is characterized by the use of certain materials. Thus, the towers are wrapped in glass, with a second skin of wood; the grand platform and the walkways are also in wood; the four lobbies under the towers are woven together with steel tapestries; and the reading rooms have red carpeting, wooden furniture, and ceilings made of great meshes of stainless steel suspended from the wall opposite the garden.

The central garden of the library emerges as the soul of the entire design, giving serenity to the complex. The towers rise with an integrity of mass characterized by an unusual use of glass as the material that best represents the unity and continuity of the surface of these volumes. The towers can be separated into two parts, the upper levels serving for storage of books and the first nine floors being used for offices. The plaza forms a decisive element of urban landscaping. From the terrace can be seen the tops of the trees of the central garden, the visible crowns of the pines that form a compact forest some six floors below. This mass of trees breathes an exuberant calm in the heart of the library.

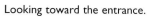

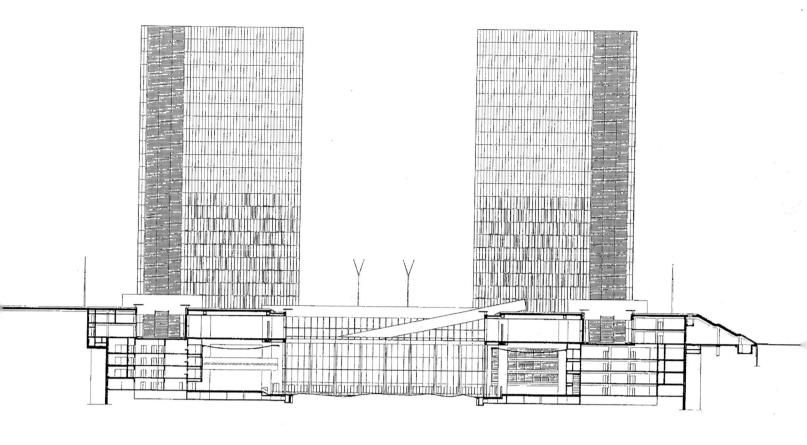

Transversal section.

The public reading rooms and exhibition halls are on the same level as the reception area, and the two floors below are dedicated to reading rooms for research and for sound and image. The library is an addition to the existing National Library dating from the 19th century. The new building can receive more than three million visitors a year and has 3,600 places for readers to sit. An exhibition center, an auditorium, conference rooms, and restaurants all add to the public dimension of the library, which will also serve as the center of the computer network linking all French public libraries. As has been said on many occasions, the new National Library is as much a new plaza for Paris as it is a new library for France.

View of the building at night.

Exterior garden.

Glass façade of the research
reading room at garden level.

View of the garden
from above.

Glass façade of one tower
with wooden shutters.

Lateral façade
of the building.

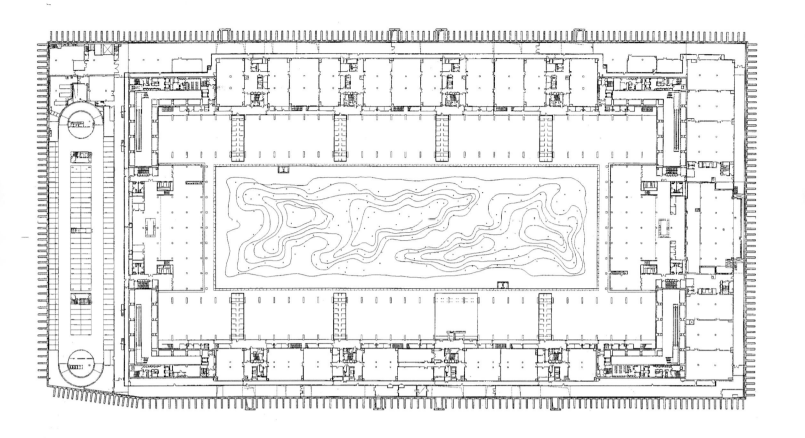

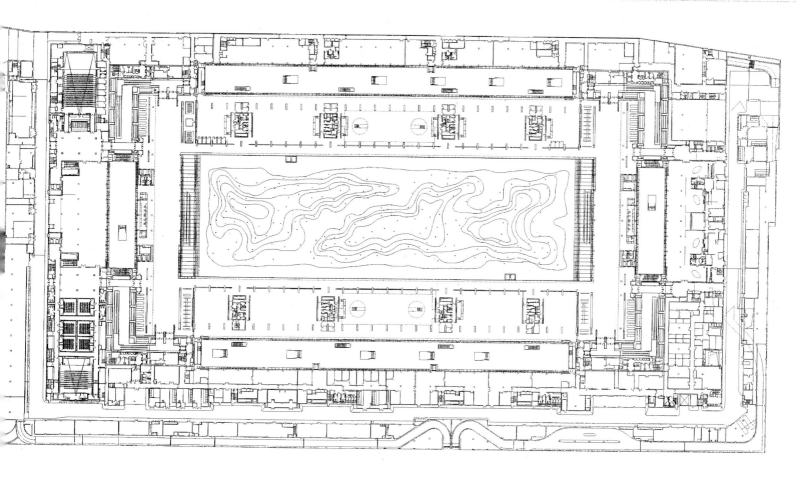

Public reading room

Lighting in the research reading room.

Information desk.

Furniture in the research
reading room.

Moving stairs in the entrance
to the towers.

Upper floors of the towers.

Torres Puerta de Europa

MADRID, 1996

As one enters Madrid from the north, the extraordinary sight of two glass towers leaning toward each other in a kind of fraternal salute is unescapable. The towers are located in a district that has expanded rapidly in recent years and has seen many new buildings erected. The 1985 *Plan General de Madrid* assigned to this particular site certain limits, which in the end suggested the possibility of building two isolated tower blocks adjacent to the Plaza Castilla. These would have to be separated by a strip of land large enough to avoid three existing metro stations and their corresponding pedestrian subways, and also to take into account access rights to an as-yet undeveloped neighboring street.

On the basis of these restrictions, architect John Burgee proposed the construction of two towers that would incline toward each other at an angle of 15 degrees and whose common meeting point would be the axis formed by the *Paseo de la Castellana*. This solution served to modify the role that the urban planners had assigned to the two blocks, and also allowed the towers to stand out from their neighbors in a unique fashion. The inclination of the towers solved the problem of the excessive separation between them, which would have diluted their impact on the profile of the city.

The face which inclines over the plaza is triangulated throughout its height with heat-laminated sections.

Ground floor, with the elevator shafts built into the interior façade. The main entrance is under the projection of the tower.

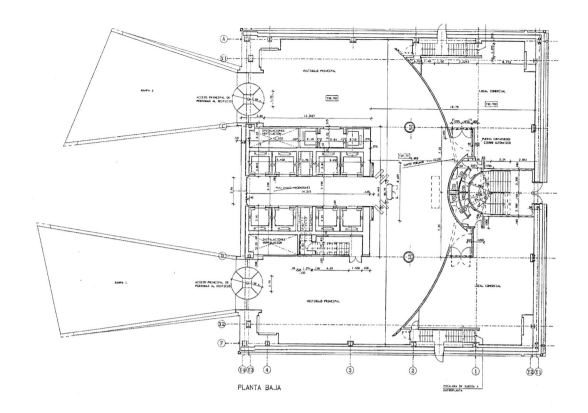

PLANTA BAJA

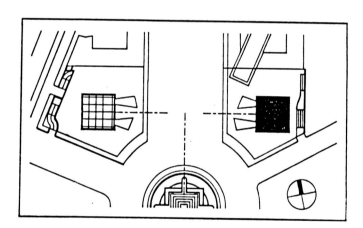

This decision to incline the towers was not only radical, however, but also inherently risky. The design of the towers' structures had to be capable not only of transmitting the vertical forces to the foundations, but also of resisting the lateral forces that would tend to demolish the buildings—the impact of the wind, and above all, the displaced force of the upper stories. The towers have a triangular framework of pillars and beams of extreme rigidity to combat lateral forces, combined with a central nucleus of concrete that acts as a huge cantilever, adding further rigidity to the structure. In addition, a series of tethered cables run up the rear façade. Finally, a series of extraordinarily rigid open-web beams distribute the horizontal forces caused by the cables.

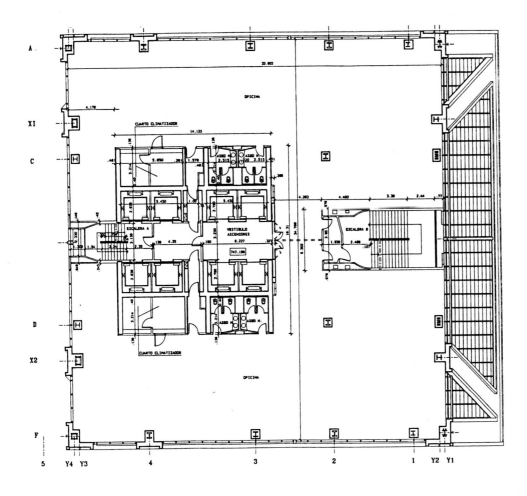

Third floor, showing the slight displacement of the elevator shafts and the section of the profiles running up the façade.

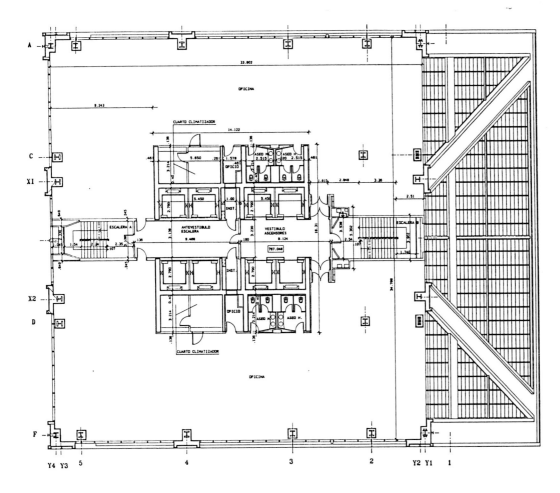

Eighth floor. The elevator shafts are situated in an intermediate position between the two façades.

Thirteenth floor, showing how, exactly halfway up the building, the elevator shafts are already being displaced toward the exterior façade.

The structure of the façade is dressed with the panels of stainless steel that characterize the complex.

The displacement between the top and bottom floors is 30 meters. A line in the lateral façade marks the area in which the two floors overlap.

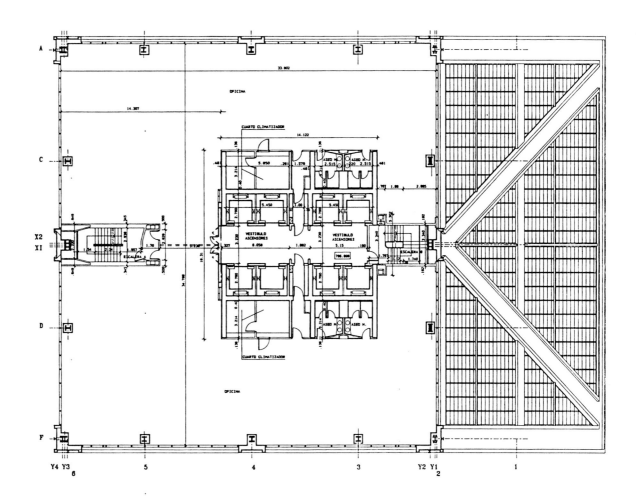

The geometry of the two towers corresponds to a parallelepiped whose base is a 35-meter square and whose height is 115 meters. Two of the faces are inclined at an angle of 14.3 degrees, meaning that the total displacement of the crown with respect to the base is almost 30 meters. This leaves only a narrow band of about 5 meters in which the base and the crown are aligned vertically, just enough to accommodate the elevator shafts and to define the vertical line of the façade. The interiors of the towers were designed to take advantage of all the space permitted by the urban plan, with three basement floors, a ground floor, a mezzanine housing technical installations, and 24 office floors, with the installations on the roof being crowned by a helicopter landing pad.

Y3   Y2

7   6   5   4   3   2   1

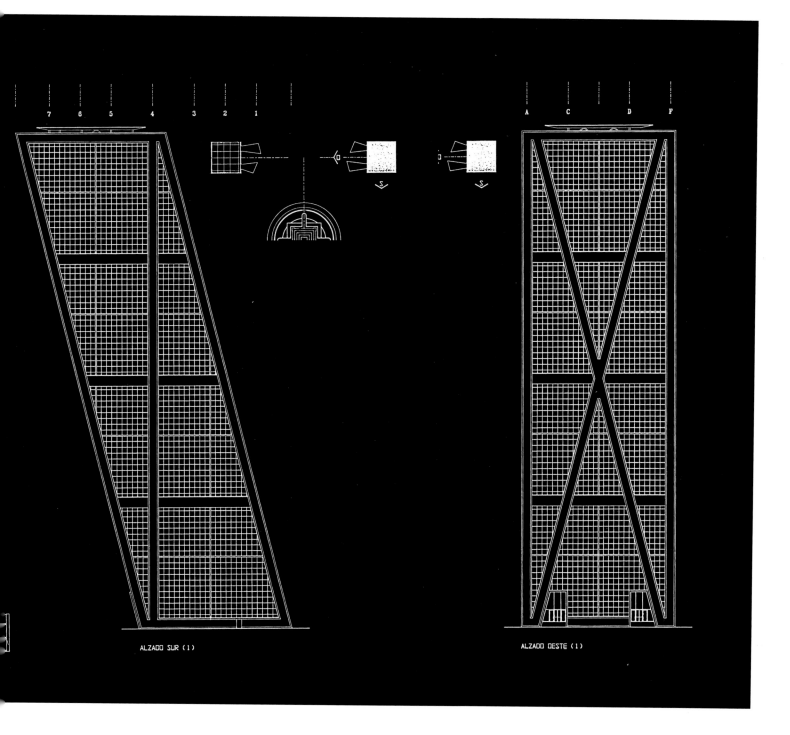

ALZADO SUR (1)   ALZADO OESTE (1)

Section through the entrance
showing the emplacement of the
two stairwells in each tower.

South and west faces, with the
helicopter landing pad looming
over the roof.

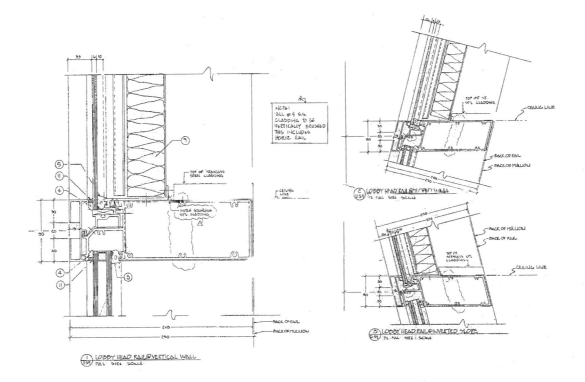

NOTE:
·ALL #4 S.S.
CLADDING TO BE
VERTICALLY BRUSHED
THIS INCLUDES
HORIZ. RAIL

TOP OF STAINLESS
STEEL CLADDING

CEILING
LINE

NOTCH STAINLESS
STL CLADDING

BACK OF RAIL
BACK OF MULLION

① LOBBY HEAD RAIL @ VERTICAL WALL
D-39 FULL SIZE SCALE

TOP OF ST.
STL CLADDING

CEILING LINE

BACK OF RAIL
BACK OF MULLION

② LOBBY HEAD RAIL @ SLOPED WALL
D-39 1/2 FULL SIZE SCALE

BACK OF MULLION
BACK OF RAIL

TOP OF
STAINLESS STL
CLADDING

CEILING LINE

③ LOBBY HEAD RAIL @ INVERTED SLOPE
D-39 1/2 FULL SIZE SCALE

Detail of the construction
showing the junction of the
glass façade with the entrance.

Various details of the
construction showing the
changes in inclination of the
aluminum window frames.

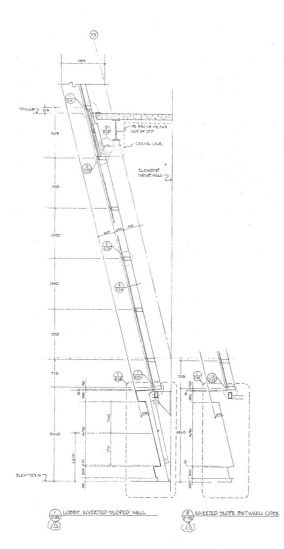

T/SLAB

IPE 330 OR IPE 360
NOT BY CFP

CEILING LINE

ELEVATOR
SHEAR WALL

① LOBBY INVERTED SLOPED WALL
D-38

② INVERTED SLOPE BETWEEN CORE

The main lobby for the elevators. The paving combines granite and marble, whose finish is of different textures.

The elevators are finished in stainless steel, marble, and lignum vitae.

Main lobby, showing the great marble partition which separates it from the shopping area.

BRUCE J. GRAHAM
SKIDMORE, OWINGS & MERRILL (SOM)

Hotel de les Arts

BARCELONA,1992

In 1985, the Barcelona City Council initiated an ambitious project for the transformation of a strategic area of the city near the historic old center and along the seashore. This immense project, sited between the industrial area of Poble Nou and the Cuidadela park has, together with the reformation of the old port area, completely opened up the city to the sea. The impetus behind the project was Barcelona's successful candidature for the 1992 Olympic Games. The area was to provide housing for the athletes and included a complete range of services, such as hotels, parks, boulevards, offices, and shopping facilities.

As well as restoring the long-neglected beaches, the project aimed to create a new residential area which would allow the citizens of Barcelona to enjoy the pleasures of the new sea front. After the Games, the athletes' residences became integrated into the rest of the city, creating a district that serves as a link between the old city and the sea. The twin towers, visible from all parts of Barcelona have become the greatest symbol of the change of the city's orientation—its opening up to the Mediterranean, whose existence seemed to be practically ignored by the layout of the city for so many years.

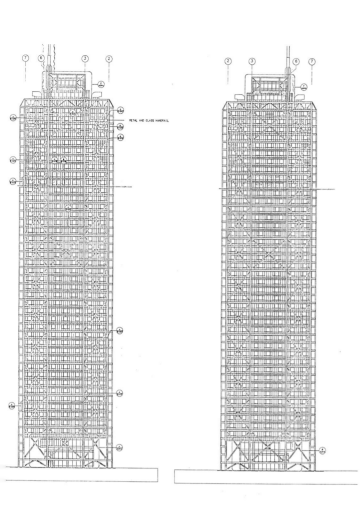

METAL AND GLASS HANDRAIL

On the previous page:

The public services which lie at the foot of the tower include restaurants, cafés, and shops, and form part of the larger leisure complex whose center is the Olympic Port.

North and south faces of the tower.

Under the shadow of the large fish designed by Frank O. Gehry, the patio around the pond is crossed by paths leading to the shopping galleries. Tree-planted terraces, reserved for clients of the hotel, make the transition from the tower to the sea.

The tower meets the lower volumes of the complex by means of a series of terraces which offer an intermediate space between the exterior and interior public areas of the hotel.

A six-story office block interrupts the view of the tower from the old center of the city, which is dominated by Montjuïc hill in the background.

Aerial view from the top of the tower. The fish, designed by the American architect Frank O. Gehry, throws shadow over the public patio that connects the lower service areas of the complex.

The hotel swimming pool, on the roof of the services area, has panoramic views of the Mediterranean sea, framed by a strange landscape of different volumes and textures.

Aerial view of the gardens, which are restricted for the use of hotel guests, and which provide an interesting filter of the Mediterranean horizon.

A number of lower volumes lie at the foot of the tower, ensuring that its transition is not too abrupt, not only with the street but also with the sea.

Arranged around a large ornamental pond are 16,000 square meters of shops, restaurants, cafés, and also a department store. Floating above all this, as if swimming in the sea itself, is a giant anodized-aluminum fish. Designed by Frank O. Gehry, the fish has become a landmark, symbolizing not only the shopping complex but also the whole strip of renewed beaches from which it is visible.

Floor plan of the entrance level.

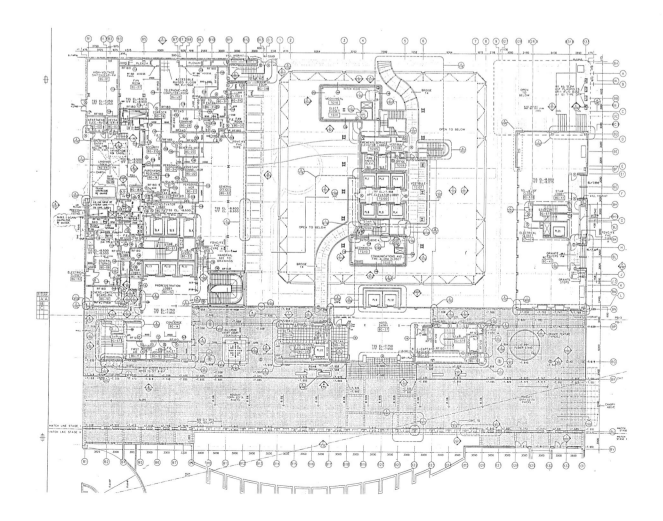

At the foot of the tower, the naked
structural skeleton is balanced over a
pond fed by a great curtain of water
from which the building seems to rise
directly. Only the indispensable lift
shafts and mechanical installations
seem to actually touch the ground.

Floor plan of the upper
basement floor.

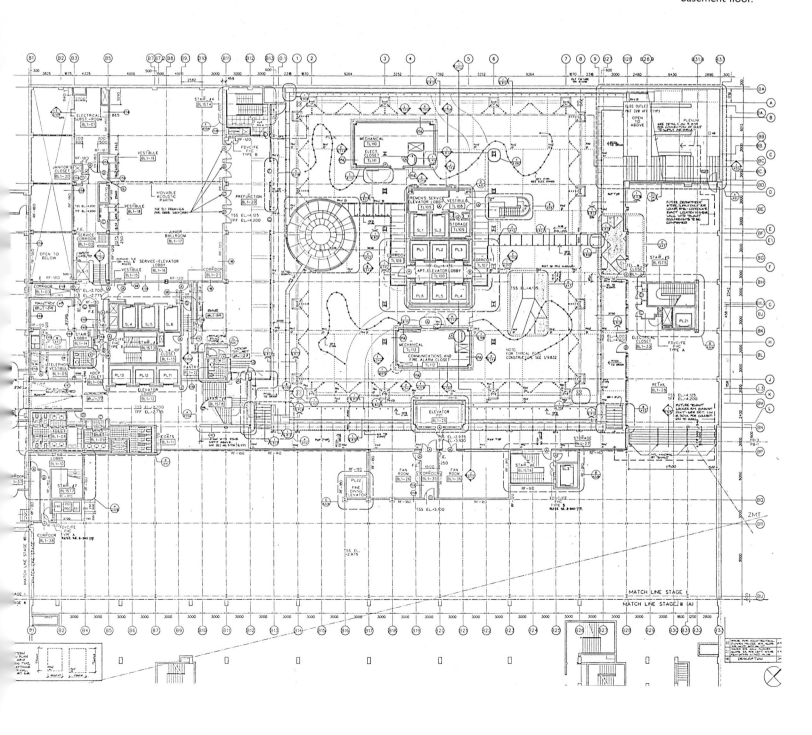

The separation of the structure of the tower from its skin creates depth in the façade; a changing interplay of light and shadow creating a richness of sights from different points of view.

Section of the complex.

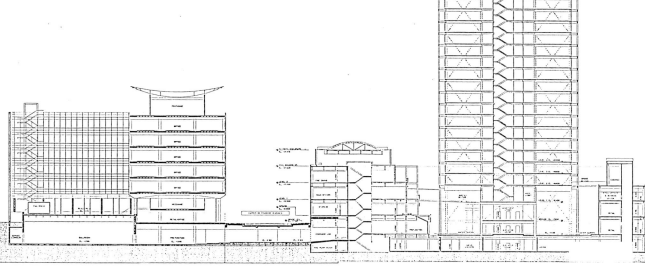

Different views of the space between the structure and the skin of the building, showing details of the various types of anchoring used and the virtual effect that the façade creates.

An 11,000-square-foot parking area is built under Francisco de Aranda street, connecting the tower with a 6-story concrete building with a glass façade. The building has almost 13,000 square feet of space available for office leasing, with a floor plan that is totally flexible. The 456 rooms of the Hotel de las Arts are complemented by restaurants, lounges, a ballroom, and a gymnasium and swimming pools located on terraces overlooking the sea. In addition to the luxury hotel, there are 29 separate apartments with private access. Well-known local artists such as Sánchez Rubio, Mateo Vilagrasa, and Miquel Rasero have collaborated in the interior design of the building, while the furniture is the work of the Catalan architect and designer Òscar Tusquets.

Tokyo City Hall

TOKYO, 1991

In November 1985, nine architectural firms were invited by the Tokyo City Council to participate in a competition for the design of a new City Hall. The old building had become outdated with regard to the needs of the enormous and sophisticated city today. In April 1986, Kenzo Tange Associates were declared the winners of the competition. The building was to be located in Shinjuku, one of the centers of Tokyo. According to the architects' plan, two aligned towers facing the park configure, together with the Assembly building, the singular functional unity of the complex.

Perhaps the most important aspect of the project is the plaza for public use. Tower I, situated between the plaza and a park, contains the governor's office, many of the administrative departments, conference rooms, and the disaster prevention center. On the thirty-third floor, the building divides into two twin towers which reach a height of 243 meters. Tower II has a height of 163 meters and is home to various agencies, public corporations and other departments.

The interior façade of the Assembly building and the colonnade supporting the corridors which connect it to Tower I delimit a wonderful urban space in which a short stretch of the street forms a vantage point over the semielliptical lower plaza.

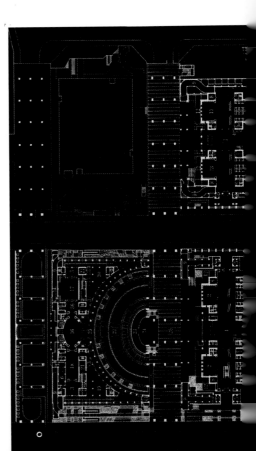

Continuity and differentiation
of the two Towers facing
the Park.

Superposition of scales, with
the Shinjuku Park Tower, also
by Kenzo Tange, repeating
the stepping of Tower II at a
greater height

East-west section of the Plaza which reveals the interplay of levels.

North-south section of the Towers on the longitudinal axis.

The park legitimates the grand scale of the Shinjuku subcenter. The Plaza gives it an urban feel.

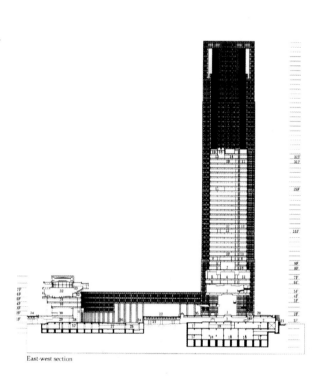

East-west section

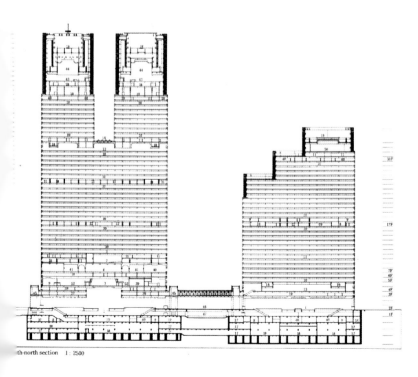

th-north section   1 : 2500

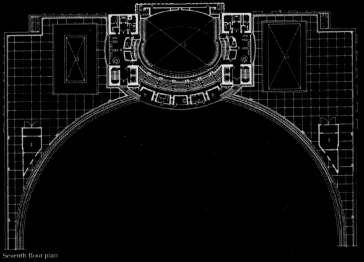

Seventh floor plan

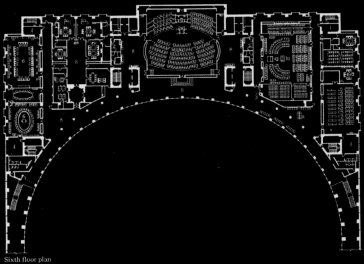

Sixth floor plan

Interplay of levels in the streets and of shadows, surfaces, and textures in the Towers.

The concavity of the Plaza turns it into an inviting urban space in the middle of a landscape of heights.

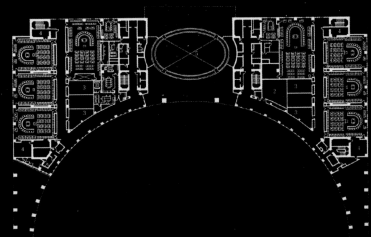

Third floor of the Assembly Building. The elliptical space over the lobby.

The Assembly is situated on the sixth floor, surrounded by the public gallery on the floor above, which projects over the Plaza.

Main west entrance to the
lobby of Tower I.

The floors are developed on the basis of a 6.4-meter grid. To gain flexibility and free space for the work place, a superstructure has been conceived for each tower formed by eight large nuclei (of 6.4 by 6.4 meters), bridged on some floors, which function as "super-girders." With a span of 19.2 meters, a spatial distribution is achieved which opens to the exterior with total freedom, surpassing the virtual perimeter defined by the nuclei. The façade, modulated with panels of 3.2 meters (half of 6.4) and 4 meters, reflects the superstructure, and its lattice-work texture lends a certain traditional character to the building as a whole.

169

The Assembly, crowning the
building, rediscovers the
elliptical shape of the lobbies.

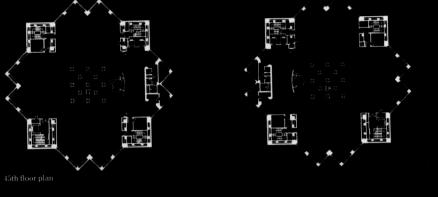
45th floor plan

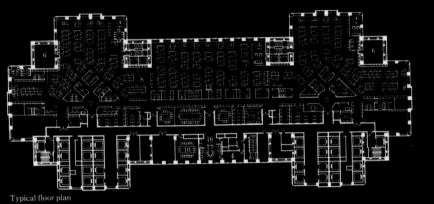
Typical floor plan

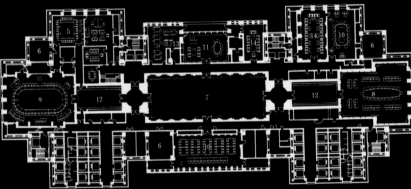
Seventh floor plan

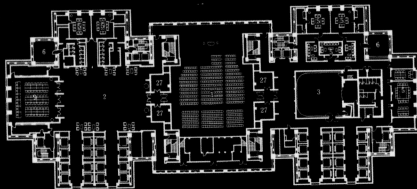
Fifth floor plan (Tower I)   1 : 1000

Umeda Sky Building

OSAKA, 1993

The skyscraper has become a universal symbol, not only of the modern city, but also of technological progress itself. Since the first examples were built in Chicago at the end of the 19th century, there has been an unstoppable race to possess the highest skyscraper in the world. However, as in all wordly things, glory is transient. Within a few years or even months, there is always another city willing to add the few extra meters needed to possess the world's tallest skyscraper.

Rather than imagining a vain attempt to build a new and shortlasting "world's highest skyscraper," the architects of Umeda Sky Building imagined an entirely new type of skyscraper consisting of two towers connected at the top. In conformity with orthodox thinking, the promoters of the project felt the need for a landmark building as a symbol for the newly created Omeda City near Osaka. They sought to design an outstanding building on an urban scale that would establish a clearly recognizable identity.

For Hara, this was a building which could serve as an image of the city of the future. The preliminary sketches contained not just two towers but a whole series of them, stretching into infinity and forming a new city, interconnected at the top. In the end, the design for the Umeda Sky Building was for two forty-story towers connected by a platform which serves as a viewpoint over the city and which Hara defines as a hanging garden.

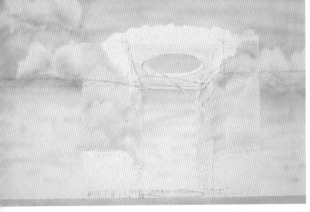

Aerial view of the complex, situated next to the Kanjo railway line that encircles the city of Osaka.

The façade of the towers, which is mainly reflective glass, acts as a mirror to the sky, the movement of the clouds and the changes of light, in an attempt to blur the solid lines that contain it.

Preliminary sketches. The idea of skyscrapers connected at their upper levels is proposed as the genesis of a new type of building capable of becoming the template of future large-scale urban development.

The ground floor of the complex. Both the front and back of the buildings contain lavishly planted spaces.

174

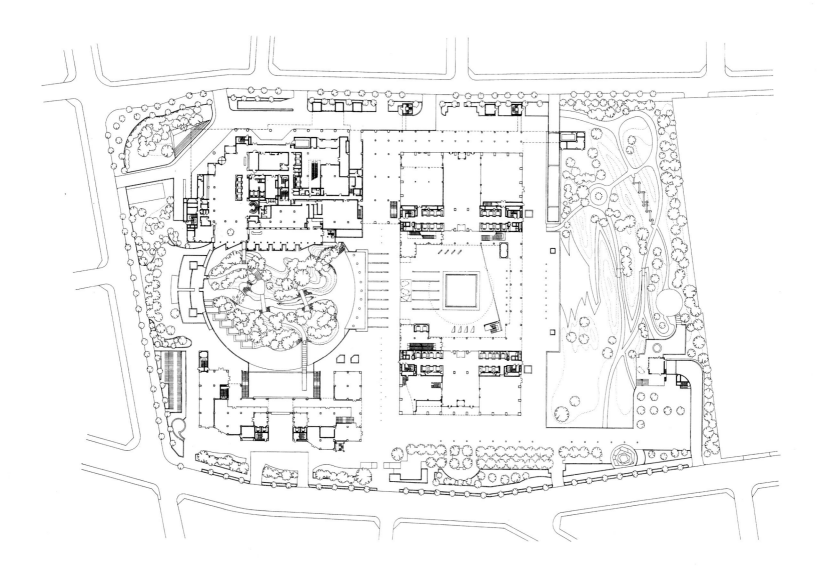

The connecting platform is perforated by a great circle which gives access to the upper viewing platform by means of two mechanical staircases suspended in space. In this way, the sky can be not only seen but also directly experienced from the access gallery, illuminated by the sun which shines through the circle. The seismic regulations governing construction in Japan are extremely restrictive, limiting the solutions and structural types that can be used. In the case of the Umeda Sky Building, the elevated platform connecting the two towers acts as an effective bracing element, aided by the intermediate bridge halfway up the building which also connects them. The building's façade is of moderately reflecting glass of near mirror quality, which captures the sky throughout its entire surface.

The contrast between new architectural images and traditional construction is patent throughout Japan, and can be seen clearly in the new Umeda Sky Building.

Second floor of the skyscrapers.

Floor plan of floors 12 to 20.

21st Floor. The intermediate bridge connecting the two towers.

View from the access gallery to the enormous hole which opens up in the platform which connects the two towers and is crossed by the two mechanical stairways which lead to the viewing platform on the top floor.

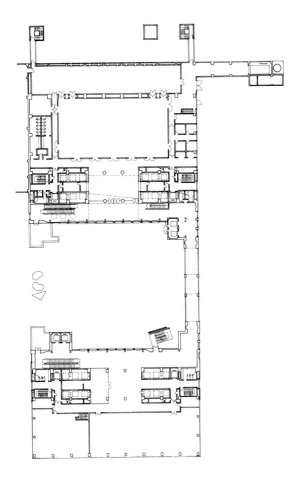

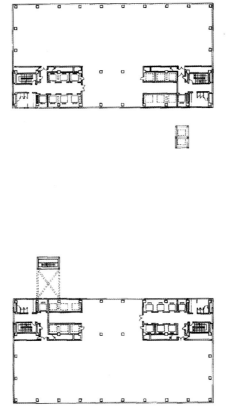

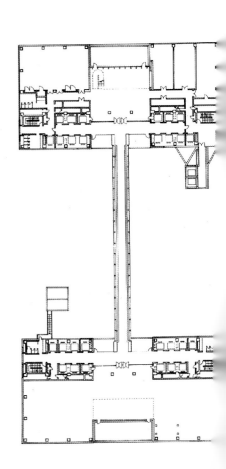

Interior lateral façade of one of the two towers of which the project is constituted.

Floor 38.
Arrival point of the mechanical stairs.

Floor 39.
Exhibition Room. Viewing platform.

Floor 40.
Open-air viewing platform. Roof.

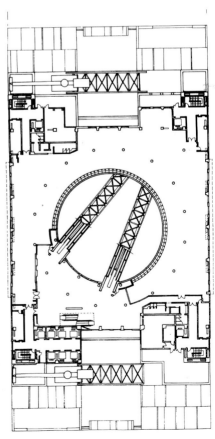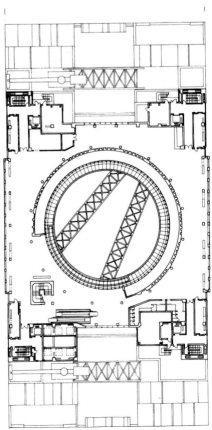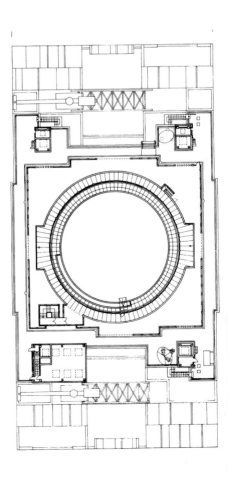

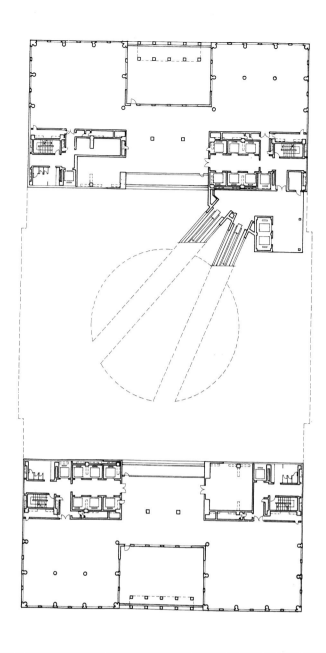

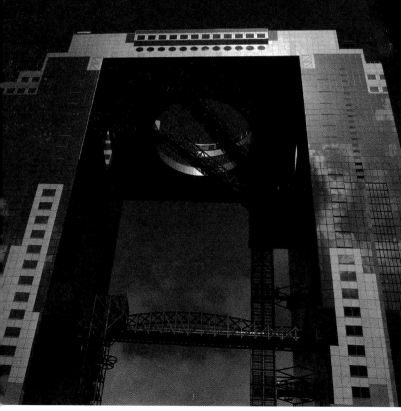

Floor 34.
From here, the two
mechanical staircases begin
to climb toward the top
floor, giving access to the
viewing platform.

View of one of the
entrances to the towers.

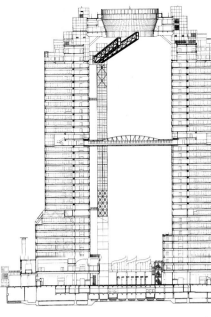

View of the intermediate
bridge connecting the two
towers on the 21st floor.

View of the stairs giving
access to the viewing
platforms on the top floors.

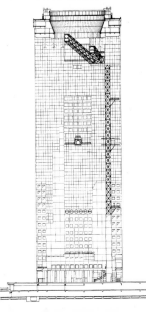

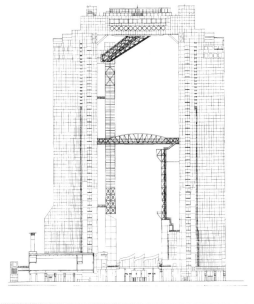

Transversal section of the building.

South face.

View of the interior of the stairs giving access to the viewing platform.

Open-air viewing platform on the top floor of the building, with its views over the city of Osaka.

Interior façades of the two towers, giving onto the central space between them.

West face.

Floor 39 where, from the indoor viewing platform, the void between the two towers can be contemplated.

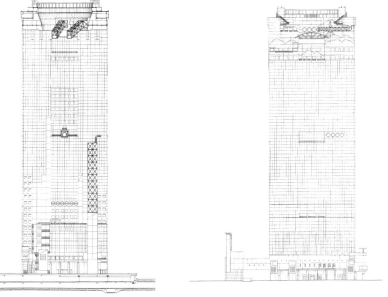

Petronas Towers

KUALA LUMPUR, 1997

In 1991, selected architects were invited to participate in an international competion to design two skyscrapers for the northeast corner of a site in the center of Kuala Lumpur. The main requirement made by the organizers of the competition was that the buildings should have a Malaysian identity. As they themselves acknowledged, however, there exists little architecture that can genuinely be called Malaysian on which to base the project. Given this requirement, the team of architects led by Cesar Pelli began with the problem of defining the qualities of distinctly Malaysian architecture.

From the first sketch onwards, the project was designed in consonance with the cultural and physical conditions existing in the country—the climate, the dominant Islamic culture, and the shapes suggested by traditional Malayan buildings and objects—while at the same time rejecting the simple option of a cultural pastiche. The most important creative decision was to make the towers symmetrical and to concentrate all the figurative and symbolic force of the project on this characteristic.

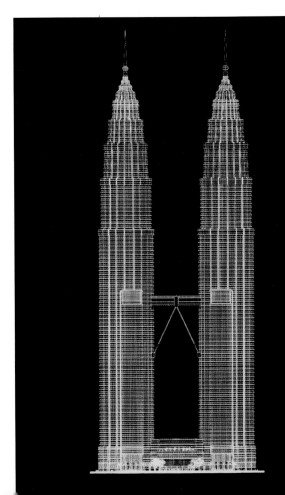

The floor plan is a result of a complex addition of basic figures that begins with the intersection of two squares, perhaps the most important geometric form in Islamic design. The use made by the architects of this geometric evolution is analogous to that used in traditional Islamic designs using simple figures to create complex patterns. At the same time, the initial squares of the floor plan are an attempt to recapture the symbolic significance of the square: the earth and its four cardinal points.

Although each tower has its own vertical axis, the overall axis of the complex is to be found in the void that lies between them, and the force of this axis is potentiated by the pedestrian bridge that connects the two 88-story towers on floors 41 and 42, where there are public observation points looking out over the city. The bridge and its supporting structure creates a gateway to heaven—a 170-meter high bridge across infinity

The Petronas Towers are sited in Kuala Lumpur, the capital of Malaysia. The tropical climate was a determining factor in deciding the façade of the buildings.

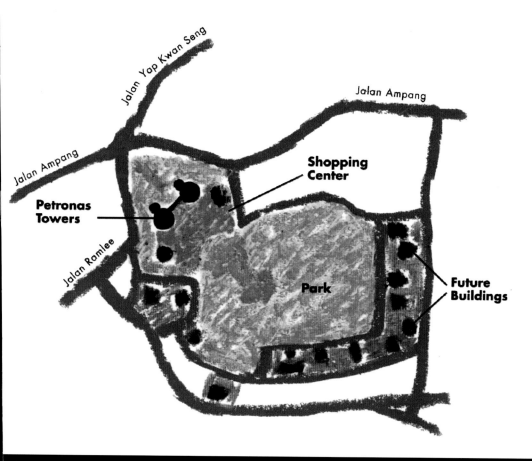

Plan of the area where the   project is sited.

Site plan of the towers together with the buildings destined for a shopping center.

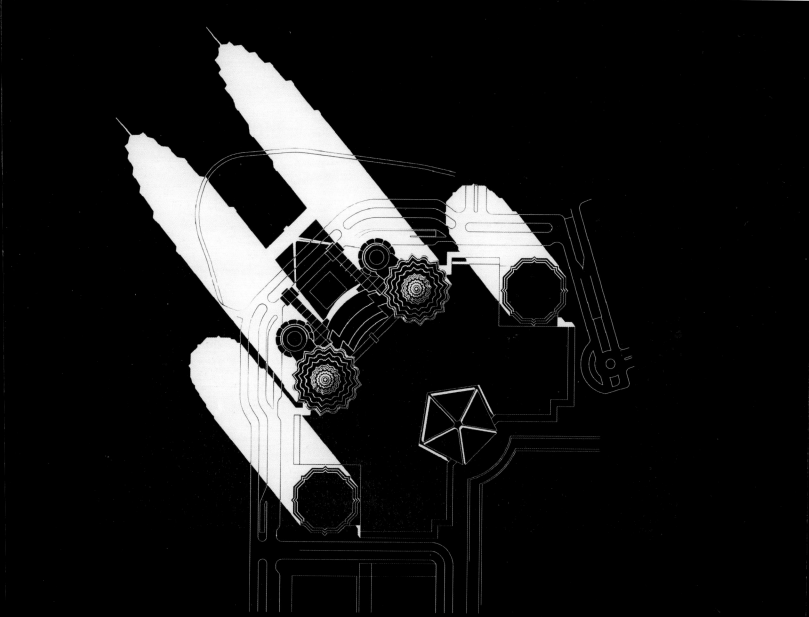

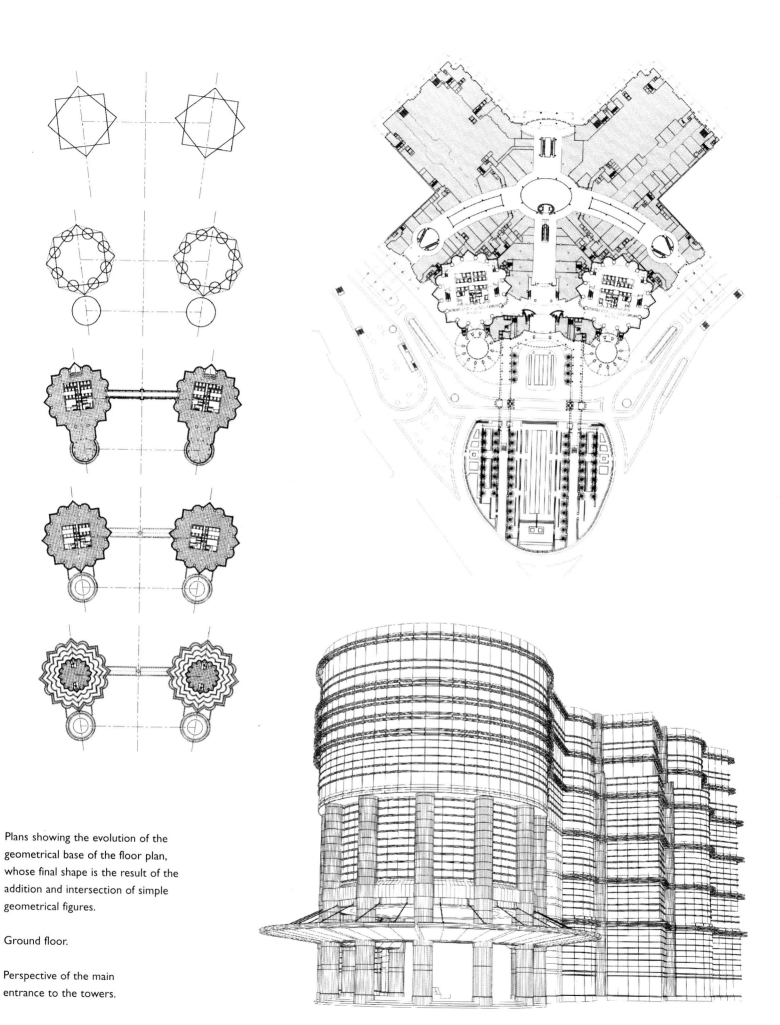

Plans showing the evolution of the geometrical base of the floor plan, whose final shape is the result of the addition and intersection of simple geometrical figures.

Ground floor.

Perspective of the main entrance to the towers.

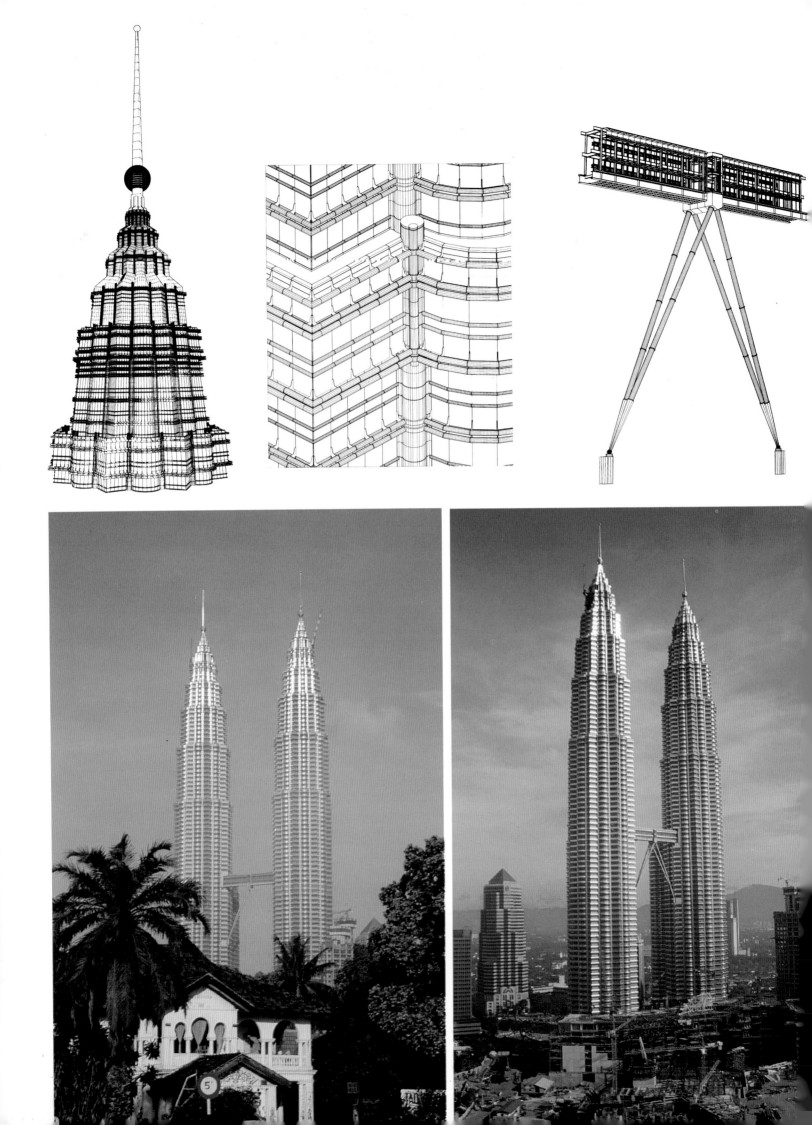

Detail of the apex.

Detail of the volumetry of the façade, designed to give protection from excessive sunlight, by means of the setting back of the floors and modifications to give more shadow.

Detail of the structure of the pedestrian bridge which connects the observation points on floors 41 and 42, looking out over the city.

The main axis of the complex lies in the void between the two towers.

The façades are of stainless steel, which amplifies the reflections caused by the bright, intense tropical light of Malaysia.

Carlos Bratke

1967 Graduated in Urban Architecture from the University of Mackenzie (FAUUM). Two years later awarded post-graduate degree in Urban Planning and Evolution by the Universidad de Sao Paulo.
1992-93 President of the IAB (Instituto de Arquitetos do Brasil). His principal works include: the church of San Pedro and San Pablo, Sao Paulo; the Concorde office block, Sao Paulo; the Morumbi Plaza shopping centre, Sao Paulo; office complex in the Avenida Luis Carlos Berrini (around 500,000 sq. metres of floor space), Sao Paulo

John Burgee & Philip Johnson
Dominguez y Martin. Arquitectos Asociados S.L.

John Burgee

1933 Chicago, (United States)
1956 Degree in architecture from the University of Notre Dame, Indiana
1958-1967 Collaborates with the Naess & Murphy studio.
Since 1967 Collaborates with Phillip Johnson.

Philips Johnson

1906 Cleveland, Ohio (United States)
1923 - 1930 Studying at Harvard University.
1943 Degree in architecture from Harvard University.
1930 - 1967 Divides his time between the Board of the Department of Architecture at the New York Museum of Modern Art (MOMA) and the professional practice as an independent architect.
Since 1967 Collaborates with John Burgee.

Burgee & Jonshon

Main works: American Telephone and Telegraph Corporate Headquarters (AT&T), New York; Cultural Center in Dade County, Miami; PPG Building, Pittsburgh; Republic Bank Center, Houston; Tycoon Towers, Virginia.

Tomas Dominguez del Castillo

193 Madrid (Spain)
1971 Degree in Architecture from the "Escuela Técnica Superior de Architectura" in Madrid (ETSAM).
Since 1971 has formed a team with J.C. Martin.

Juan Carlos Martín Baranda

1941 San Sebastian (Spain)
1971 Degree in Architecture from the "Escuela Técnica Superior de Architectura" in Madrid (ETSAM).
Since 1971 has formed a team with T. Dominguez.

Domínguez y Martín

Main works: Faculty of Computer Engineering at the Autonomous University of Madrid.; 114 dwelling building, Valladolid; the Castilla Plaza Transport Exchange, Madrid; IBM Headquarters, Madrid; Faculty of Philosophy and Arts.

Sir Norman Foster

1935 Born in Manchester (U.K.)
1961 Graduated in Architecture from Manchester University.
1967 Founded Foster Associates together with Wendy Foster.
1968-83 Collaborated in various projects with Buckminster Fuller.
1967-90 Offices for the Hongkong and Shanghai Bank in Hongkong.
1990 Founded Sir Norman Foster & Partners.
Recent Projects (**1990-97**): Stanstead Airport; Century Tower, Tokyo; Carré d'Arts, Nîmes; University of Cranfield Library; Law Faculty, Cambridge; Joselyn Art Museum, Nebraska.

T.H. Hamzah & Yeang Sdn. Bhd

Founded in **1976**, the firm has offices in Kuala Lumpur and Penang, and has specialised in the construction of buildings that combine height and energy saving measures.
1990-95 Recent projects: Development Plan for the Kota Kinabalu Sports Complex and Park; designs and direction of development plan for the TAS Industries buildings, Kuala Kuantan; Bumiputra Bank Training Centre, Bangi; Fima Timuran factory, Trengganu.

Tengku Robert Hamzah

Born in **1939**.
1971 Graduated in Architecture from the Architectural Association School, London.
1972-76 Worked in the studio of Pakatan Akitek.
1976 Formed T.R. Hamzah & Yeang Sdn. Bhd, in association with Ken Yeang.

Ken Yeang

Born in Penang (Malaysia)
1971 Graduated in Architecture from the Architectural Association School, London.
1975 Doctorate in Architecture from Cambridge University.
1976 Formed T.R. Hamzah & Yeang Sdn. Bhd., in association with Tengku Robert Hamzah.

Hiroshi Hara. Atelier Φ

Atelier Φ

1936 Born in Kawasaki (Japan).
1961 Master's degree in Architecure from the University of Tokyo.
1964 Doctorate in Architecture from the University of Tokyo.
1970- Working in association with the architectural group Atelier Φ
Main projects: Art Museum, Tasaki; Yamamoto International; JR central train station, Kyoto; secondary school, Ose.

Helmut Jahn, FAIA

1940 Born in Nuremburg (Germany)
1965 Graduated from the Technische Hochschule of Munich.
1967 Graduated from the Illinois Institute of Technology.
1967 Takes up position in C. F. Murphy Associates.
1982 President of Murphy/Jahn.
Projects built between 1985-90: 362 West Street, Durban; North Western Atrium Center, Chicago; Park Avenue Tower, New York; O'Hare Airport.
Recent projects (**1990-97**): Livingston Plaza, New York; Two Liberty Place, Philadelphia; 120N. LaSalle Street, Chicago; One American Plaza, San Diego; Hyatt Regency Roissy, Paris; Munich Center Order; Hitachi Tower, Singapore; Caltex House, Singapore; Kempinski Hotel, Munich; Ku-Damn, Berlin.

Kohn, Pedersen & Fox
William Pedersen

1961 Graduated in Architecture from the University of Minnesota, U.S.A.
1968 Master of Architecture from the Massachusetts Institute of Technology, U.S.A.
1965 Roman Prize from the American Academy of Rome.
1976 Co-founder of Kohn Pedersen Fox, New York.
1982-89 Visiting Professor in various American and Japanese Universities.
1986 Eero Sarinen Professor, Yale University.
Main Projects: Proctor and Gamble General Offices Complex, Cincinnati; Rockefeller Plaza West, New York; World Bank, Washington DC; United States Courthouse, Portland.

KISHO KUROKAWA

1934 Born in Nagoya (Japan).
Graduate in Architecture from the University of Tokyo.
1960 Co-founder of the Metabolist Movement.
1981 Honourary Member of the American Institute of Architects.
1986 Honourary Member of the Royal Institute of British Architects. Gold Medal of the French Academy.
1987 Awarded the Japanese literary Grand Prix upon the publication of "Philosophy of Symbiosis".
1992 Prize of the Japan Art Academy for his Photography Museum in Nara, Japan.
Recent Projects: Lane Crawford Place, Singapore; Pacific Tower, Paris; Photography Museum, Nara; Modern Art Museum, Wakayama.

NIKLEN SEKKEI

1900 Founding of Nikken Sekkei Ltd. in Tokyo.
With its three main offices in Tokio, Osaka and Nagoya, Nikken Sekkei is a consulting firm specialising in architectural projects, landscape design and the supervision of urban projects and services on a world-wide scale. During the firm's existence it has participated in more than 13,000 projects in more than 40 countries, both in the private and public sectors, and employs more than 200 specialists in Japan alone, constituting one of the largest architectural consulting firms in the world. As well as 10 further branches in Japan, it has offices in Seoul, Kuala Lumpur and Shanghai, and is affiliated with many of the most prestigious architectural and consulting firms throughout the world.
Recent projects: Osaka World Trade Center, Osaka; Bunyo Civic Center, Tokyo; Solid Square, Tokyo:

CESAR PELLI & ASSOCIATES INC
CESAR PELLI - FRED W. CLARKE

CESAR PELLI

Born in Argentina, he graduated in Architecture from the University of Tucuman.
A study grant enabled him to travel to the U.S.A. where he worked for 10 years in the studio of Eero Saarinen.
1968-1976 Partner of Gruen Associates, Los Angeles.
1977 Elected Dean of the Yale School of Architecture. Founded Cesar Pelli & Associates.
The firm's recent projects include the World Financial Center, New York; Norwest Tower, Minneapolis; enlargement of the Pacific Design Center, Los Angeles; Mattatuck Museum, Waterbury, Conneticut.

FRED W. CLARKE

1970 Graduated in Architecture from the University of Texas in Austin. Commenced working for Gruen Associates, Los Angeles, together with Cesar Pelli.
1977 Founded Cesar Pelli & Associates in conjunction with Cesar Pelli.

RAFAEL PELLI

1985 Master in Architecture from the University of Harvard.
1986-89 Employed by Hardy Holzman Pfeiffer Associates, New York.
1989 Joins Cesar Pelli & Associates.

DOMINIQUE PERRAULT

1953 Clermont-Ferrand (France)
1978 Degree in Architecture from the Paris University of Architecture.
1979 Town planning studies at the National School of Bridges and Highways, Paris.
1980 Degree in History from the School of Higher Education in Social Studies.
1982 - 1984 Works at APUR.
1985 Founds his own professional Studio.
Recent projects: water-treatment plant, Ivry-sur-Seine; 93 dwelling building, Groupe André, Paris; Swimming Pool and Cycling track, Berlin.

ROCCO SEN-KEE YIM

1952 Born in Hong Kong.
1976 Graduated in Architecture from the University of Hong Kong.
1979 Created Rocco Design Associates.
1982 Member of RIBA.
Recent projects: First Prize in the international competition for the Bastille Opera, Paris; Lok Fu Shopping Center II, Lok Fu; Beijing Silver Tower, Beijing; Ambassador Hotel, Hong Kong.

SKIDMORE, OWINGS & MERRILL (SOM)

BRUCE J. GRAHAM
1948 Graduated in Architecture from the University of Pennsylvania, Trustee, U.S.A.
1949 Recruited by the architectural firm Skidmore, Owings & Merrill (SOM), Chicago, U.S.A.
1960 Made full partner of SOM.
His designs have been built in many countries, including the U.S.A., Great Britain, Guatemala, Indonesia, Saudi Arabia, Korea, Egypt and Spain. They include the John Hancock Center, Chicago; Sears Tower, Chicago; One Financial Place, Chicago; Canary Wharf, London.

ADRIAN D. SMITH

1969 Graduated in Architecture from the University of Illinois, Chicago.
1969 Joined Skidmore, Owings & Merrill (SOM), where, as Design Partner he has carried out numerous projects.
Recent projects: Xiamen Posts and Telecommunications building, Xiamen, China; South Point East-West, Miami; Washington University, St. Louis, Missouri; 10 Fleet Place, Ludgate, London.

KENZO TANGE ASSOCIATES

1913 Born in Japan.
1938 Graduated in Architecture from the University of Tokyo, Japan.
1945 Master of Architecture from the University of Tokyo.
1946 Founds his own studio in Tokyo.
1985 Establishes Kenzo Tange Associates Urbanists and Architects, with branches in Tokyo, Paris, New York, Singapore and Riyadh.
1987 Pritzer Prize for Architecture, U.S.A.
Has been Visiting Professor and Doctor Honoris Causa in Univesities in Europe, America and Asia.
Recent projects. Shinjuku Park Tower, Tokyo; Gran Ecran building, Paris; Fuji-Sankei Communications Group building, Tokyo.

CALVIN TSAO

1952 Born in Hong Kong.
1974 Graduated in Architecture from the University of California, Berkeley, U.S.A.
1979 Master of Architecture from the Harvard Graduate School of Design, Columbia University, U.S.A.
After working for I.M. Pei & Partners, becomes part of the firm of Richard Meier & Associates.
1985 Founding of Tsao & Mckown Architects, New York, U.S.A.
Recent projects: residential building of 28 storeys in Shanghai; Menara IMC 30-storey office block, Kuala Lumpur.

ZACK MCKOWN

1952 Born in South Carolina, U.S.A.
1974 Graduated in Architecture from the University of South Carolina, U.S.A.
1978 Master of Architecture, Harvard Graduate School of Design , Columbia University, U.S.A.
Joins the firm of Ulrich Franzen & Associates, New York.
1980 Joins Rafael Viñoly & Associates.
1985 Founding of Tsao & McKown Architects, New York, U.S.A.
Principal projects: residential building of 28 storeys in Shanghai; Menara IMC 30-storey office block, Kuala Lumpur.